THE HAZARDOUS EARTH

LANDSLIDES

Mass Wasting, Soil, and Mineral Hazards

Timothy Kusky, Ph.D.

Facts On File
An imprint of Infobase Publishing

LANDSLIDES: Mass Wasting, Soil, and Mineral Hazards

Copyright © 2008 by Timothy Kusky, Ph.D.

Facts On File, Inc.
An imprint of Infobase Publishing
132 West 31st Street
New York NY 10001

Library of Congress Cataloging-in-Publication Data

Kusky, Timothy M.
    Landslides: mass wasting, soil, and mineral hazards / Timothy Kusky.
        p. cm.—(Hazardous Earth)
    Includes bibliographical references and index.
    ISBN-13: 978-0-8160-6465-6
    ISBN-10: 0-8160-6465-2
    1. Landslides—Juvenile literature. 2. Mass wasting—Juvenile literature. 3. Landslide hazard analysis—Juvenile literature. I. Title.
    QE599.A2.K87 2008
    551.32'07—dc22   2007024674
         ·307   ×C
                              0 = 14476996

Facts On File books are available at special discounts when purchased in bulk quantities for businesses, associations, institutions, or sales promotions. Please call our Special Sales Department in New York at (212) 967-8800 or (800) 322-8755.

You can find Facts On File on the World Wide Web at http://www.factsonfile.com

Text design by Erika K. Arroyo
Illustrations by Richard Garratt
Photo research by Suzanne M. Tibor

Printed in the United States of America

VB ML 10 9 8 7 6 5 4 3 2 1

This book is printed on acid-free paper and contains 30 percent post-consumer recycled content.

*To the Philippine villagers of the island of Leyte who were buried
by a massive landslide on February 17, 2006*

■ ■ ■

Contents

Preface

Natural geologic hazards arise from the interaction between humans and the Earth's natural processes. Recent natural disasters such as the 2004 Indian Ocean tsunami that killed more than a quarter million people and earthquakes in Iran, Turkey, and Japan have shown how the motion of the Earth's tectonic plates can suddenly make apparently safe environments dangerous or even deadly. The slow sinking of the land surface along many seashores has made many of the world's coastal regions prone to damage by ocean storms, as shown disastrously by Hurricane Katrina in 2005. Other natural Earth hazards arise gradually, such as the migration of poisonous radon gas into people's homes. Knowledge of the Earth's natural hazards can lead one to live a safer life, providing guidance on where to build homes, where to travel, and what to do during natural hazard emergencies.

The eight-volume The Hazardous Earth set is intended to provide middle- and high-school students and college students with a readable yet comprehensive account of natural geologic hazards—the geologic processes that create conditions hazardous to humans—and what can be done to minimize their effects. Titles in the set present clear descriptions of plate tectonics and associated hazards, including earthquakes, volcanic eruptions, landslides, and soil and mineral hazards, as well as hazards resulting from the interaction of the ocean, atmosphere, and land, such as tsunamis, hurricanes, floods, and drought. After providing the reader with an in-depth knowledge of naturally hazardous processes, each volume gives vivid accounts of historic disasters and events that have shaped human history and serve as reminders for future generations.

One volume covers the basic principles of plate tectonics and earthquake hazards, and another volume covers hazards associated with volcanoes. A third volume is about tsunamis and related wave phenomena, and another volume covers landslides, soil, and mineral hazards, and includes discussions of mass wasting processes, soils, and the dangers of the natural concentration of hazardous elements such as radon. A fifth volume covers hazards resulting from climate change and drought, and how they affect human populations. That volume also discusses glacial environments and landforms, shifting climates, and desertification—all related to the planet's oscillations from ice ages to hothouses. Greater understanding is achieved by discussing environments on Earth that resemble icehouse (glaciers) and hothouse (desert) conditions. A sixth volume, entitled *The Coast,* includes discussion of hazards associated with hurricanes, coastal subsidence, and the impact of building along coastlines. A seventh volume, *Floods,* discusses river flooding and flood disasters, as well as many of the contemporary issues associated with the world's diminishing freshwater supply in the face of a growing population. This book also includes a chapter on sinkholes and phenomena related to water overuse. An eighth volume, *Asteroids and Meteorites,* presents information on impacts that have affected the Earth, their effects, and the chances that another impact may occur soon on Earth.

The Hazardous Earth set is intended overall to be a reference book set for middle school, high school, and undergraduate college students, teachers and professors, scientists, librarians, journalists, and anyone who may be looking for information about Earth processes that may be hazardous to humans. The set is well illustrated with photographs and other illustrations, including line art, graphs, and tables. Each volume stands alone and can also be used in sequence with other volumes of the set in a natural hazards or disasters curriculum.

Acknowledgments

Many people have helped me with different aspects of preparing this volume. I would especially like to thank Carolyn, my wife, and my children, Shoshana and Daniel, for their patience during the long hours spent at my desk preparing this book. Without their understanding this work would not have been possible. Frank Darmstadt, executive editor, reviewed and edited all text and figures, providing guidance and consistency throughout. The excellent photo research provided by Suzie Tibor is appreciated, and she is responsible for locating most of the excellent photographs in this volume. Many sections of the work draw from my own experiences doing scientific research in different parts of the world, and it is not possible to thank the hundreds of colleagues whose collaborations and work I have related in this book: Their contributions to the science that allowed the writing of this volume are greatly appreciated. I have tried to reference the most relevant works or, in some cases, more recent sources that have extensive reference lists. Any omissions are unintentional.

Introduction

The outermost layer of the Earth consists of rock, soil, organic matter, and other materials that together are called *regolith. Landslides* examines the formation of soil from regolith and underlying bedrock and discusses some of the hazardous elements that are concentrated in soils. Its later chapters examine the physical characteristics of the regolith and emphasize what happens when large sections of the regolith move, either slowly by creeping along or more suddenly in landslides and *avalanches.*

Most interactions between people and the Earth involve this regolith, so it is essential that a complete understanding of its characteristics be obtained. The regolith forms by the breakdown of solid bedrock, through processes of *chemical, biological,* and *mechanical weathering,* and the complete transition between bedrock and soil is included in the definition. The regolith contains many different minerals and also many concentrations of elements that are hazardous to humans. Different physical conditions, such as changes in water content, temperature, slope, and pressure control how the regolith behaves. In some situations, the regolith is a stable layer of soil upon which farms, towns, and cities are built. In other cases, the regolith is slowly expanding and contracting, and, in many places, the regolith is slowly creeping downhill. In rare dramatic examples, large sections of regolith and even bedrock may suddenly collapse and race downhill in *landslides* and related phenomena. This book addresses hazards related to all these different aspects of the regolith.

Some materials found in the *soil profile* and the regolith are dangerous to humans. Natural geologic processes have concentrated some of the more hazardous elements and compounds in some locations and left them virtually absent in others. Many of these hazards are silent killers. Poisonous gases creep into homes, dissolved chemicals make their way into *groundwater* wells, and radioactive particles are constantly shooting through our bodies. *Landslides* explains the physical processes that cause hazardous elements to be concentrated in some cases and what needs to be done to minimize the hazards associated with geologic materials.

Toxic metals, such as selenium, zinc, arsenic, lead, and other elements, may be concentrated in some locations and make their way through soils to drinking water supplies, food supplies, and even into the air. Exposure to toxic levels of these and other trace elements is a serious global health issue with billions of people exposed to potentially harmful material hazards. *Landslides* provides an in-depth understanding of where these and other elements are naturally concentrated, as well as what the effects of removing them from the environment, such as during lead-mining operations, may be on human health. An emerging field of science is *medical geology,* which deals with the effects of geologic materials and processes on human, plant, and animal health. Although the effects of airborne and trace quantities of some hazardous materials have only recently been appreciated, some of the harmful effects of certain minerals have been known for thousands of years. Aristotle noted lead poisoning in some lead miners, and Hippocrates described relationships between environmental hazards and human health.

Asbestos is presently being removed from thousands of buildings because of the perceived threat it poses to people exposed to breathing its deadly fibers. Asbestos is a fire retardant and was widely used as an additive to insulation materials until it was determined that breathing asbestos fibers could cause cancer. Asbestos, however, is relatively inert and does not tend to leap into the air system as many fear. If left alone, asbestos poses little threat to those walking past insulated pipes and the like. However, if asbestos becomes airborne as fine-grained dust particles, it can be deadly. Other dusts can carry pathogens, toxins, soil fungi, heavy metals, and other harmful elements that can adversely affect human health.

Landslides examines other materials that are hazardous in other ways. For instance, there are many clays that expand by 400 percent when water is added to their environment. The expansion of these clays is powerful and has the force to slowly crumble bridges, foundations, and tall buildings. Damage from expanding clays is one of the most costly of all natural hazards in the United States, causing billions of dollars of damage every year.

Invisible and odorless poisonous gases that are emitted from underlying rocks, minerals, and soils invade many homes and businesses in the United States and abroad. The most common hazardous gas of this class is *radon*, which can cause lung cancer and other ailments. Millions of homes in the United States have radon problems, and the populace is beginning to understand and deal with this problem.

Natural and human causes of groundwater contamination are discussed. On the Indo-Gangetic plain, south of the Himalayan Mountains in India and Bangladesh, many groundwater wells are contaminated with natural arsenic. This water is drunk by 25 to 75 million people, who are suffering from the awful effects of arsenic poisoning. Much of this suffering is preventable. It is a simple matter to get water from nearby, uncontaminated wells. However, many of the local people do not understand the danger and cannot afford the energy to walk the extra distance to get the water from a clean well. Monitoring groundwater arsenic levels could prevent much of this poisoning, and this is being done by several U.N. organizations with limited success. Getting drinking water in many parts of the world is not as simple as turning on a faucet in the United States. Somebody must carry vessels from the home to the well, fill the vessels, and carry them back to the home. Some wells are simple and easily accessed; others involve long climbs down treacherous paths in narrow caves that lead to the groundwater level.

Landslides investigates natural and human-induced processes related to geologic materials that are hazardous on local and global scales. For instance, thousands of underground fires are burning in underground coal seams, especially in China. These fires release tons of hazardous gases to the atmosphere and may be contributing to global warming. Some estimates suggest that the amount of carbon dioxide released by underground coal fires in China is about equal to all of the carbon dioxide released by cars and trucks in the United States.

Mass wasting is the movement of soil, rock, and regolith downslope by gravity without the direct aid of a transporting medium such as ice, water, or wind. It is estimated that more than 2 million mass movements occur each year in the United States alone. Mass movements occur at various rates, from a few inches per year to sudden catastrophic rockfalls and avalanches that can bury entire towns under tons of rock and debris. In general, the faster the mass movement, the more hazardous it is to humans. However, even slow movements of soil down hills can be extremely destructive to buildings, pipelines, and other constructions.

In the United States alone, mass movements kill people and cost more than \$1.5 billion a year. Other mass movements overseas have killed tens to hundreds of thousands of people in a matter of seconds. Mass wasting occurs under a wide variety of environmental conditions and forms a continuum with weathering, as periods of intense rain reduce friction between regolith and bedrock, making movement easier. Mass movements also occur underwater, such as the giant submarine landslides associated with the 1964 Alaskan *earthquake.*

Mass movements are a serious concern in hilly or mountainous terrain, especially for buildings, roads, and features engineered into hillsides. Mass movements are also a problem along riverbanks and in places with large submarine escarpments, such as along deltas like the Mississippi in Louisiana. The problems are further compounded in areas prone to seismic shaking or severe storm-related flooding. *Landslides* provides an in-depth analysis of the causes and effects of different kinds of mass wasting processes, and how people can reduce their risk from these hazards. Less spectacular but common effects of slow downhill mass movements are the slow tilting of telephone poles along hillsides and slumping of soil from oversteepened embankments onto roadways during storms.

Mass wasting is becoming more of a problem as the population moves from the overpopulated flatland to new developments in hilly terrain. In the past, small landslides in the mountains, hills, and canyons were not a serious threat to people, but now, with large numbers of people living in landslide-prone areas, landslide hazards and damage are rapidly increasing.

The first chapter in this book examines the processes of weathering and the production of regolith and soil from solid bedrock. The second chapter provides an in-depth analysis of the different types of harmful elements that are concentrated in some places in the regolith, and the third chapter discusses contamination of groundwater and changes in physical properties of soils with the addition of water. The role of water in the expansion and contraction of soils is also discussed. The fourth chapter examines the physical forces that drive the movement of regolith downhill and the different processes that are involved in mass wasting. The fifth chapter focuses on undersea landslides. The sixth chapter presents a series of examples of mass wasting disasters, with different triggers including earthquakes, volcanic eruptions, and storms. The seventh chapter includes information on what can be done to reduce the risks and damages from mass wasting processes.

1

Weathering and the Formation of Soils

"Mass wasting" is defined as the downslope movement of products of weathering, and there is a continuum between the processes of weathering, erosion, and mass wasting. Weathering is a process of mechanical and chemical alteration marked by the interaction of the *lithosphere*, atmosphere, hydrosphere, and biosphere. The resistance to weathering varies with climate, composition, texture, and how much a rock is exposed to the elements. Weathering processes occur at the lithosphere/atmosphere interface. This is actually a zone that extends down into the ground to the depth that air and water can penetrate. In some regions, this is a few feet, in others a half mile or more. In this zone, the rocks make up a porous network, with air and water migrating through cracks, fractures, and pore space. The effects of weathering can often be seen in outcrops on the side of roads, where the road cuts through the zone of alteration into underlying bedrock. These roadcuts and weathered outcroppings of rock show some similar properties. The upper zone near the surface is made of soil or regolith in which the texture of the fresh rock is not apparent, the middle zone shows the rock altered, but retaining some of its organized appearance, and the lower zone consists of fresh unaltered bedrock.

Processes of Weathering

There are three main types of weathering. Chemical weathering is the decomposition of rocks through the alteration of individual mineral

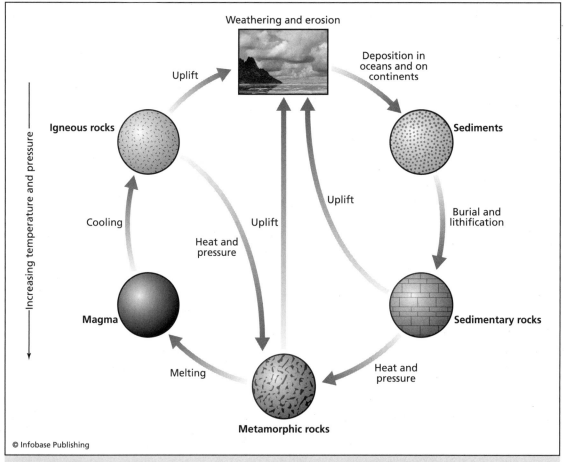

Diagram illustrating the different processes involved in the rock cycle. Uplift of igneous, metamorphic, or sedimentary rocks to the surface exposes them to weathering and erosion, where they form soils and sediments. These soils and sediments eventually get buried, turn into sedimentary rocks, and start the rock cycle all over again.

grains and is a common process in the soil profile. Mechanical weathering is the disintegration of rocks, generally by abrasion. Mechanical weathering is common in the talus slopes at the bottom of the mountains, along the beach, and along river bottoms. Biological weathering involves the breaking down of rocks and minerals by biological agents. Some organisms attack rocks for nutritional purposes; for instance, chitons bore holes through limestone along the seashore, extracting their nutrients from the rock.

In general, mechanical and chemical weathering are the most important, and they work hand in hand to break down rocks into regolith. The combination of chemical, mechanical, and biological weathering produces soils, or a weathering profile.

MECHANICAL WEATHERING

There are several different types of mechanical weathering that may act separately or together to break down rocks. The most common process of mechanical weathering is abrasion, where movement of rock particles in streams, along beaches, in deserts, or along the bases of slopes causes fragments to knock into each other. These collisions cause small pieces of each rock particle to break off, gradually rounding the particles and making them smaller, and creating more surface area for processes of chemical weathering to act on.

Some rocks develop *joints,* or parallel sets of fractures, from differential cooling, from the pressures exerted by overlying rocks, or from tectonic forces. Joints are fractures along which no observable movement has occurred. Joints promote weathering in two ways. First, they are planes of weakness across which the rock can break easily, and second, they act as passageways for fluids to percolate along, promoting chemical weathering.

Crystal growth may aid mechanical weathering. When water percolates through joints or fractures, it can precipitate minerals such as salts, which grow larger and exert large pressures on the rock along the joint planes. If the blocks of rock are close enough to a free surface such as a cliff, large pieces of rock may be forced off in a rockfall, initiated by the gradual growth of small crystals along joints.

Water's volume increases by 9 percent when it freezes to form ice. Water is constantly seeping into the open spaces provided by joints in rocks. When water filling the space in a joint freezes, it exerts large pressures on the surrounding rock. These forces are very effective agents of mechanical weathering, especially in areas with freeze-thaw cycles. They are responsible for most rock debris on *talus* slopes of mountains.

Heat may also aid mechanical weathering, especially in desert regions where the daily temperature range may be extreme. Rapid heating and cooling of rocks sometimes exerts enough pressure on them to shatter them to pieces, thus breaking large rocks into smaller fragments.

Plants and animals may also aid mechanical weathering. Plants grow in cracks and push rocks apart. This process may be accelerated if trees become uprooted or are blown over by wind, exposing more of the underlying rock to erosion. Burrowing animals, worms, and other

A large slab of rock broken off from the top of a mountain in Alaska by ice wedging. The block is about to fall into the valley below, forming a rockfall, and will then spread out as shattered boulders on the talus slope at the base of the mountain. *(T. Kusky)*

organisms bring an enormous amount of chemically weathered soil to the surface and continually turn the soils over and over, greatly assisting the weathering process.

CHEMICAL WEATHERING

Minerals that form in *igneous rocks* and metamorphic rocks at high temperatures and pressures may be unstable at temperatures and pressures at the Earth's surface, so they react with water and atmosphere to produce new minerals. This process is known as chemical weathering. The most effective chemical agents are weakly acidic solutions in water. Therefore, chemical weathering is most effective in hot and wet climates.

Rainwater mixes with carbon dioxide from the atmosphere and from decaying organic matter, including smog, to produce carbonic acid according to the reaction:

$$H_2O + CO_2 \rightarrow H_2CO_3$$
Water + carbon dioxide → carbonic acid

Carbonic acid ionizes to produce the hydrogen ion (H^+), which readily combines with rock-forming minerals to produce alteration products. These alteration products may then rest in place and become soils or be eroded and accumulate somewhere else.

Hydrolysis occurs when the hydrogen ion from carbonic acid combines with K-feldspar to produce kaolinite, a clay mineral, according to the reaction:

$$2\ KAlSi_3O_8 + 2\ H_2CO_3 + H_2O \rightarrow Al_2Si_2O_5(OH)_4 + 4\ SiO_2 + 2\ K^{+1} + 2\ HCO_3$$

feldspar + carbonic acid + water → kaolinite + silica + potassium +
bicarbonate ion

This is one of the most important reactions in chemical weathering. The product, kaolinite, is common in soils and is virtually insoluble in water. The other products, silica, potassium, and bicarbonate, are typically dissolved in water and carried away during weathering.

Much of the material produced during chemical weathering is carried away in solution and deposited elsewhere, such as in the sea. The highest-temperature minerals are leached the easiest. Many minerals combine with oxygen in the atmosphere to form another mineral, by oxidation. Iron is very easily oxidized from the Fe+2 state to the Fe+3 state, forming goethite or, with the release of water, heamatite.

$$2FeO + OH \rightarrow Fe_2O_3 + H_2O$$

Different types of rock weather in different ways. For instance, *granite* contains K-feldspar and weathers to clays. Building stones are selected to resist weathering in different climates, but now increasing acidic pollution is destroying many old landmarks. Chemical weathering results in the removal of unstable minerals and a consequent concentration of stable minerals. Included in the remains are quartz, clay, and other rare minerals such as gold and diamonds, which may be physically concentrated in placer deposits.

On many boulders, weathering only penetrates a fraction of its diameter, resulting in a rind of the altered products of the core. The thickness of the rind itself is useful for knowing the age of the boulder, if rates of weathering are known. These types of weathering rinds are useful in determining the age of rock slides and falls and the time interval between rockfalls in any specific area.

Exfoliation is a weathering process where rocks spall off in successive shells, like the skin of an onion. Exfoliation is caused by differential stresses within a rock formed during chemical weathering processes. For instance, feldspar weathers to clay minerals, which take up a larger volume than the original feldspar. When the feldspar turns to clay, it exerts considerable outward stress on the surrounding rock, which forms fractures parallel to its surface. This need for increased space is accommodated by minerals through the formation of these fractures, which cause rocks on the hillslope or mountain to be detached and susceptible to sliding or falling in a mass wasting event.

If weathering proceeds along two or more sets of joints in the subsurface, it may result in shells of weathered rock that surround unaltered rocks, looking like boulders. This is known as *spheroidal weathering.* The presence of several sets of joint surfaces increases the effectiveness of chemical weathering, because the joints increase the available surface area to be acted on by chemical processes. The more subdivisions within a given volume, the greater the surface area. Climate is also an important factor in how fast weathering proceeds, as explained in more detail in the sidebar on Cleopatra's Needle.

Spheroidal weathering in Qaidam Basin, northwestern China. The rounded boulders are formed in place by the weathering away of material from between the boulders, where water percolated along several perpendicular sets of joint planes.

HOW FAST IS CHEMICAL WEATHERING?
THE EXAMPLE OF CLEOPATRA'S NEEDLE

Chemical weathering operates on surfaces and is especially effective where acidic rainwater can interact with and alter minerals such as feldspar, changing them into soft clay. The clay is much softer than the original minerals and gets easily washed away by rain, completing the chemical weathering process. Chemical weathering happens at different rates in different climates. For instance, in deserts with virtually no rainfall, chemical weathering will be very slow, whereas in wet climates, especially where rain is more acidic, chemical weathering will be fast. This difference is well illustrated by the case of Cleopatra's Needles, a trio of Egyptian obelisks taken from the Sahara and exported to New York, London, and Paris.

Cleopatra's Needles are each 68 feet (21 m) high and were built in the ancient Egyptian city of Heliopolis for Pharaoh Thutmose III, around 1450 B.C.E. They were cut from granite that is exposed in Upper Egypt near Aswan and inscribed with extensive hieroglyphs. The needles experienced a long history, being inscribed by new hieroglyphs by Ramses II in 1250 B.C.E., moved to the Mediterranean port of Alexandria by the Romans around 12 B.C.E., and used as part of the Caesarium during the brutal reign of Augustus Caesar. Soon after they were erected in Alexandria, the needles were toppled and buried in sand for many generations, shielding the faces and hieroglyphs from chemical weathering.

After the opening of the Suez Canal in Egypt in 1869, Ismail Pasha, the khedive of Egypt, made a gift of one of the obelisks to the United States, hoping to expand trade relations. The gift was formally transmitted by his son, Tewfik Pasha, in 1879 and then erected in New York's Central Park in 1881. The move of the needle from Alexandria to New York was financed by the railroad magnate William Vanderbilt and logistically coordinated by Henry Gorringe, a lieutenant commander of the U.S. Navy. The 244-ton needle was moved on the steamship *Dessoug,* shipped across the Mediterranean Sea and the Atlantic Ocean on the ship's deck. The obelisk was so big that it took four months to transport it from the banks of the Hudson River to the park. A trestle bridge was specially built from New York's Fifth Avenue to Greywacke Knoll in Central Park, just behind the Metropolitan Museum of Art.

Since the erection of the needle in Central Park in 1881, the hieroglyphs and inscriptions have experienced a greatly accelerated rate of chemical weathering. The inscriptions that lasted 3,500 years in the desert have, in a little more than 100 years, been essentially removed by the more intense chemical weathering in the moist chemically active climate of New York. The acid rain that characterizes New England has changed the feldspars on the outer inch of the obelisk to clay, which then has washed away. Some mechanical weathering has also played a role, in that the freeze-thaw cycle from the cold winters in New York allows ice to form in the clay minerals, forcing the clay and feldspars off the surface. The hieroglyphs that were inscribed by the Egyptian pharaohs, endured the Roman occupation, and sat undisturbed in the Sahara for 3,500 years could not survive a century in the chemically tough environment of New York.

BIOLOGICAL WEATHERING

Biological weathering is the least important category of weathering. In some places, plants and microorganisms derive nutrition from dissolving minerals in rocks and soil, thus contributing to their breakdown and weathering. There are enormous numbers of microorganisms and insects living in the soil horizon, and these contribute to the breakdown of organic material in the soils and also contribute their tests, or bodies, when they die. Biological weathering may also include some of the effects of roots pushing rocks apart or expanding cracks in the weathered rock horizon. These effects also move rock fragments, so they are discussed under mechanical weathering.

Factors That Influence Weathering

The effectiveness of weathering processes is dependent upon several factors, explaining why some rocks weather one way in one location and a different way in another. Rock type is an important factor in determining the weathering characteristics of a hillslope, because different minerals react differently to the same weathering conditions. For instance, quartz is resistant to weathering, and quartz-rich rocks typically form large mountain ridges. Conversely, shales readily weather to clay minerals, which are easily washed away by water, so shale-rich rocks often occupy the bottoms of valleys. Examples of topography being closely related to the underlying geology in this manner are abundant in the Appalachians, Rocky Mountains, and most other mountain belts of the world.

Wedging and uplift of rock slab by tree roots, California *(USGS)*

Rock texture and structure are important in determining the weathering characteristics of a rock mass. Joints and other weaknesses promote weathering by increasing the surface area for chemical reactions to take place on, as previously described. They also allow water, roots, and mineral precipitates to penetrate deeply into a rock mass, exerting outward pressures that can break off pieces of the rock mass in catastrophic rockfalls and slides.

The slope of a hillside is also important in determining what types of weathering and mass wasting processes occur there. Steep slopes let the products of weathering get washed away, whereas gentle slopes promote stagnation and the formation of deep weathered horizons. Differ-

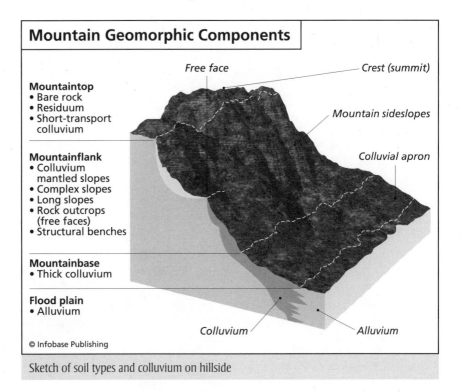

Mountain Geomorphic Components

Free face

Crest (summit)

Mountaintop
• Bare rock
• Residuum
• Short-transport
  colluvium

Mountain sideslopes

Mountainflank
• Colluvium
  mantled slopes
• Complex slopes
• Long slopes
• Rock outcrops
  (free faces)
• Structural benches

Colluvial apron

Mountainbase
• Thick colluvium

Flood plain
• Alluvium

Colluvium

Alluvium

© Infobase Publishing

Sketch of soil types and colluvium on hillside

ent types of soils are found on slopes than on valley floors in places with the same climate and underlying rock types.

Climate is one of the most important factors in determining how a site weathers. Moisture and heat promote chemical reactions, so chemical weathering processes are strong, fast, and dominate mechanical processes in hot, wet climates. In cold climates, chemical weathering is much less important. Mechanical weathering is very active during freezing and thawing, so mechanical processes such as ice wedging tend to dominate chemical processes in cold climates. These differences are exemplified by two examples of weathering. In much of New England, a hike over mountain ridges will reveal fine, $\frac{1}{10}$-inch thick striations that were formed by glaciers moving over the region more than 10,000 years ago. Chemical weathering has not removed even these very thin marks in 10,000 years. In contrast, new construction sites in the Tropics, such as roads cut through mountains, often expose fresh bedrock. In a matter of 10 years, these road cuts will be so deeply eroded to a red, soil-like material called gruse that the original rock will not be recognizable.

As in most things, time is important. It takes tens of thousands of years to wash away glacial grooves in cold climates, but in the Tropics weathered horizons that extend to several hundred feet may form over a few million years. These variations are important when considering the mass wasting processes.

Formation of Soils

Differences in *soil profile* and type result from differences in climate, the originating rock type, the types of vegetation and organisms, topography, and time. Normal weathering produces a characteristic soil profile,

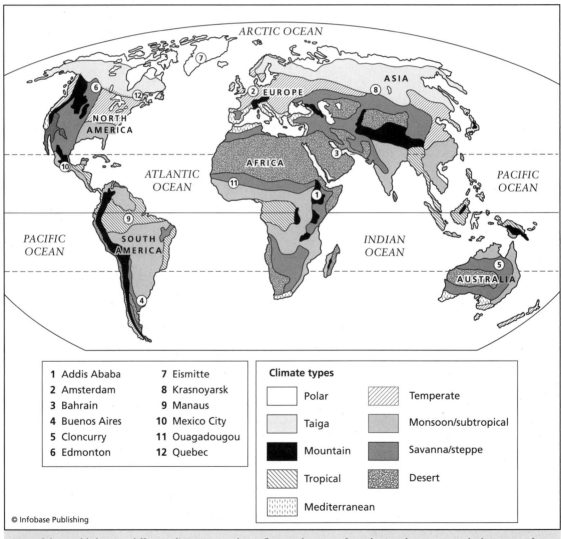

1 Addis Ababa	7 Eismitte
2 Amsterdam	8 Krasnoyarsk
3 Bahrain	9 Manaus
4 Buenos Aires	10 Mexico City
5 Cloncurry	11 Ouagadougou
6 Edmonton	12 Quebec

Climate types

Polar	Temperate
Taiga	Monsoon/subtropical
Mountain	Savanna/steppe
Tropical	Desert
Mediterranean	

© Infobase Publishing

Map of the world showing different climate zones that influence the type of weathering that occurs and what types of soils develop in a region

marked by a succession of distinctive horizons in a soil from the surface downward. The A-horizon is closest to the surface and typically has a gray or black color because of high concentrations of *humus* (decomposed plant and animal tissues). The A-horizon has typically lost some substances through downward leaching. The B-horizon is typically brown or reddish, enriched in clay produced in place and transported

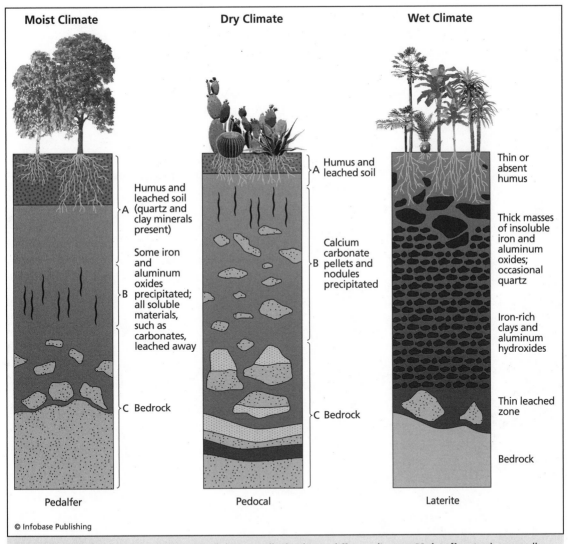

Diagram illustrating the different types of soil that typically develop in different climates. **Moist climates** have a well-developed A-horizon with high concentrations of humus and a heavily leached B-horizon. **Dry climates** have soils with thin or absent A-horizons and calcium carbonate concentrated in the B-horizon. **Wet climates** are characterized by thin or absent humus and A-horizons, with underlying thick masses of insoluble iron and aluminum oxides.

downward from the A-horizon. The C-horizon of a typical soil consists of slightly weathered parent material. Young soils typically lack a B-horizon, and the B-horizon grows in thickness with increasing age.

Some unusual soils form under unusual climate conditions. Polar climates are typically cold and dry, and the soils produced there are typically well drained without an A-horizon, sometimes underlying layers of frost-heaved stones. In wetter polar climates, tundra may overlie permafrost, which prevents the downward draining of water. These soils are saturated in water and rich in organic matter. These polar soils are very important for the global environment and global warming. They have so much organic material in them that is effectively isolated from the atmosphere that they may be thought of as locking up much of the carbon dioxide on the planet. Cutting of northern forests, as is going on in Siberia, may affect the global carbon dioxide budget, possibly contributing to climate change and global warming.

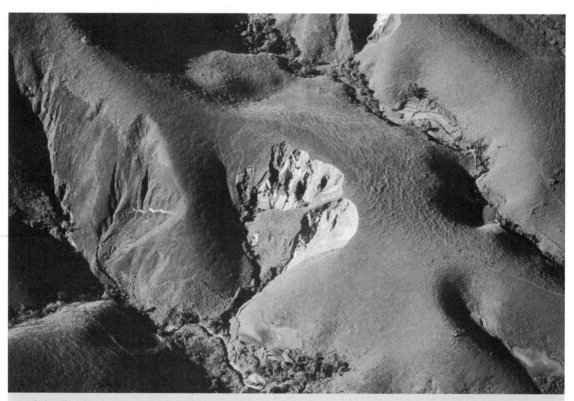

Eroded gullies (known as *lavakas*) on deforested slopes in Madagascar. These gullies form rapidly during the rainy season, often after the soil profile beneath a surface crust has eroded, causing the surface to collapse catastrophically into the gully. *(Corbis)*

Dry climates limit the leaching of unstable minerals such as carbonate from the A-horizon, which may also be enhanced by evaporation of groundwater. Extensive evaporation of groundwater over prolonged time leads to the formation of caliche crusts. These are hard, generally white carbonate minerals and salts that were dissolved in the groundwater, but got precipitated when the groundwater moved up through the surface and evaporated, leaving the initially dissolved minerals behind.

In warm wet climates, most elements except aluminum and iron are leached from the soil profile, forming laterite and bauxite. Laterites are typically deep red in color and are found in many tropical regions. Bauxites are aluminum-rich soils, formed by intense weathering and leaching away of other soil elements. Some of them are so hard that they are used for bricks.

Soils form at various rates in different climates and conditions, ranging from about 50 years in moderate temperatures and wet climates to 10,000 to 100,000 years for a good soil profile to develop in dry climates. Some soils, such as those in the Tropics, have been forming for several million years and are quite mature. Deforestation causes erosion of soils, which cannot be reproduced quickly. In many places, such as Madagascar, South America, and Indonesia, deforestation has led to accelerated rates of soil erosion, removing thick soils that have been forming for millions of years. These soils supported a rich diversity of life, and it is unlikely that the soils will ever be restored in these regions.

Conclusion

Regolith and soil form by the chemical, mechanical, and biological breakdown of solid bedrock. Many environmental factors determine which types of soils may form in any particular place, with climate, slope, and underlying geology playing the largest roles. Soils mature at different rates in different climates, with thick tropical soils forming faster than soils in cold dry climates. Many soils have an A-horizon on the surface, with a high concentration of organic material. The B-horizon underlies the A-horizon and receives material leached from the A-horizon. The C-horizon consists of slightly weathered parent material, and the D-horizon is the relatively unaltered bedrock.

2

Hazardous Elements in Soils and the Regolith

Natural processes in soils and the regolith in many places on the planet concentrate potentially hazardous geologic materials. The hazards to people that are posed by these elements depend on the ways they interact with their environment, which differs greatly between cultures. Primitive cultures that live off the land are more susceptible to hazards and diseases associated with contaminated or poor water quality, toxic elements in plants harvested from contaminated soils, and insect- and animal-borne diseases associated with unsanitary environments. In contrast, more developed societies are more likely to be affected by air pollution, a different kind of water pollution, and indoor pollution such as radon exposure. Some diseases reflect a complex interaction between humans, insects or animals, climate, and the natural concentration of some elements in the environment. For instance, schistosomiasis-bearing snails are abundant in parts of Africa and Asia where natural waters are rich in calcium derived from soils, but in similar climates in South America, schistosomiasis is rare. It is thought that this difference is because the waters in South America are calcium poor and the disease-bearing snails need the calcium to build their shells.

All life that we know is built from a few basic elements, including hydrogen, carbon, nitrogen, oxygen, phosphorous, sulfur, chlorine, sodium, magnesium, potassium, and calcium. Some other elements are important for life, as they play vital roles in controlling how tissues and organs work. Trace element metals are present in very dilute quantities in our bodies, and some that are known to be important for life functions include fluorine, chromium, manganese, iron, cobalt, copper, zinc, selenium, molybdenum, and iodine. Other elements accumulate in tissue as it ages, but their function, and whether they are beneficial or detrimental, is yet to be determined. These *age elements* include nickel, arsenic, aluminum, and barium.

The distribution of elements in the natural environment is complex and may be changed by many different processes. Geologic processes such as volcanism may concentrate certain elements in some locations even to ore-grade or unhealthy levels. When igneous rocks are weathered, the concentrations of specific elements may be increased or decreased in the soil horizon, depending on the element, climate, and other factors. After this, biologic processes may further concentrate elements. Together, processes of leaching and accumulation of elements during soil formation, biological concentration, and many other processes may concentrate or disperse elements that may be harmful to humans.

This chapter examines the processes that concentrate hazardous elements in soils and how these elements make it into homes and human bodies and cause harm to individuals and whole populations.

Hazardous Elements, Minerals, and Materials

There are more than 100 naturally occurring elements, many of which are toxic to humans in high doses and some of which occur in the regolith in high concentrations. The same elements may be beneficial or even necessary in small dilute doses and pose little or no threat in intermediate concentrations. Most elements show similar toxicity effects on people, although not all are necessary in small doses nor are they all toxic in high doses. Understanding the effects of trace elements in the environment on human health is the realm of the huge and rapidly growing field of medical geology and is beyond the scope of this book. A few specific examples can be instructive.

Some minerals are hazardous when exposed in the natural environment or when extracted in mining operations. In particular, selenium, asbestos, silica, coal dust, and lead can be harmful when inhaled or when present in high concentrations in the environment. These are discussed next, along with the beneficial mineral iodine.

Iodine

Iodine occurs naturally in the geologic environment and is released from rocks by weathering. It is readily soluble in water, so most iodine makes its way to the sea after it is leached from bedrock or soil. A deficiency of iodine in the body can lead to several adverse health effects including thyroid disease and goiter.

There is a strong correlation between the geography of occurrence of thyroid disease and a deficiency of iodine in the environment. Much of the northern half of the conterminous United States has soils with low iodine contents, and it is the same region that yields most of the thyroid disease cases in the United States.

Selenium

Selenium is one of the most toxic elements known in the environment. Like most elements, selenium is needed in small concentrations for normal biological functions. Concentrations of 0.04 to 0.1 parts per million are healthy, but any concentrations over 4 parts per million are toxic.

Selenium is produced naturally by volcanic activity and usually ejected as small particles that land near the volcano, resulting in a concentration near volcanic vents. Selenium in natural soils ranges from 0.1 parts per million to more than 12,000 parts per million in organic-rich soils. Selenium exists in insoluble form in acidic soils and in soluble form in alkaline soils. Selenium may also be concentrated by biological activity. Some plants take up soluble selenium and concentrate it in their structures. The efficiency of this process is dependent on what form (soluble or insoluble) selenium exists in the environment. Selenium is also concentrated in human tissue to about 1,000 times the background level in freshwater. It is also concentrated by up to 2,000 times the natural background level in marine fish.

The concentration of selenium in biologic material has persisted through geological time, and many coals and fossils fuels are also rich in selenium. Burning coal releases large amounts of selenium, which then rains down on the landscape.

Asbestos

Asbestos was widely used as a flame retardant in buildings through the mid-1970s and is present in millions of buildings in the United States. It was also used in vinyl flooring, ceiling tiles, and roofing material. It is no longer used in construction since it was recognized that it might cause certain types of diseases, including asbestosis (pneumoconiosis), a chronic lung disease. Asbestos particles get lodged in the lungs and the lung tissue hardens around them, decreasing lung capacity. This

Asbestos mine in Zimbabwe (formerly Rhodesia) in 1959 *(Getty)*

decreased lung capacity causes the heart to work harder, leading to heart failure and death. Virtually all deaths from asbestosis can be attributed to long-term exposure to asbestos dust in the workplace before environmental regulations governing asbestos were put in place. A less common disease associated with asbestos is mesothelioma, a rare cancer of the lung and stomach linings. Asbestos has become one of the most devastating occupational hazards in U.S. history, costing billions of dollars in cleanup of schools, offices, homes, and other buildings. Approximately $3 billion a year is currently spent on asbestos removal in the United States.

Asbestos is actually a group of six related minerals, all with similar physical and chemical properties. Asbestos includes minerals from the amphibole and serpentine groups that are long and needle-shaped, making it easy for them to get lodged in people's lungs. The Occupational Safety and Health Administration (OSHA) defined asbestos as having dimensions of greater than 5 micrometers (0.002 inches) long, with a length to width ratio of at least 3:1. The minerals in the amphibole group included in this definition are grunerite (known also as amosite), reibeckite (crocidolite), anthophyllite, tremolite, and actinolite, and the serpentine group mineral that fits the definition is chrysotile. Almost all of the asbestos used in the United States is chrysotile (known as white asbestos), and about 5 percent of the asbestos used was crocidolite (blue asbestos) and amosite (brown asbestos). There is currently considerable debate among geologists, policymakers, and medical officials on the relative threats from different kinds of asbestos.

In 1972, OSHA and the U.S. government began regulating the acceptable levels of asbestos fibers in the workplace. The Environmental Protection Agency (EPA) declared asbestos a Class A carcinogen. The EPA composed the Asbestos Hazard Emergency Response Act, which was signed by President Reagan in 1986. OSHA gradually lowered the acceptable limits from a preregulated estimate of greater than 4,000 fibers per cubic inch (1,600 fibers per cubic centimeter) to 4 fibers per cubic inch (1.6 fibers per cubic centimeter) in 1992. Responding to public fears about asbestosis, Congress passed a law requiring that any asbestos-bearing material that appeared to be visibly deteriorating must be removed and replaced by non–asbestos-bearing material. This remarkable ruling has resulted in billions of dollars being spent on asbestos removal, which in many cases may have been unnecessary. The asbestos can only be harmful if it is an airborne particle, and only long-term exposure to high concentrations leads to disease. In some cases, it is estimated that the processes of removing the asbestos resulted in the inside air becoming more hazardous than before removal, as the remediation can cause many small particles to become airborne and fall as dust throughout the building.

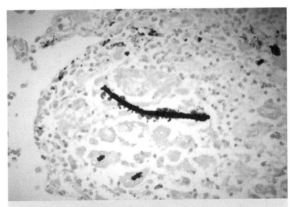

Ferruginous body (likely an asbestos fiber) in a lung tissue sample, highlighted using Prussian blue iron stain. Ferruginous bodies are microscopic particles coated with an iron-protein complex and surrounded by macrophages. These particles are often found to be asbestos fibers. *(Photo Researchers, Inc.)*

Asbestos fibers in the environment have led to some serious environmental disasters, as the hazards were not appreciated during early mining operations before the late 1960s. One of the worst cases occurred in the town of Wittenoom, Australia. Crocidolite was mined in Wittenoom for 23 years between 1943 and 1966, and the mining was largely unregulated. Asbestos dust filled the air of the mine and the town, and the 20,000 people who lived in Wittenoom breathed the fibers in high concentrations daily. More than 10 percent, or 2,300, of the people who lived in Wittenoom have since died of asbestosis, and the Australian government has condemned the town and is in the process of burying it in deep pits to rid the environment of the hazard.

In the United States, W. R. Grace and Company in Libby, Montana, afflicted hundreds of people with asbestos-related diseases through mining operations. Vermiculite was mined at Libby from 1963 to 1990 and shipped to Minneapolis to make insulation products, but the vermiculite was mixed with the tremolite (amphibole) variety of asbestos. In 1990, the EPA tested residents of Libby and found that 18 percent of residents who had been there for at least six months had various stages of asbestosis and that 49 percent of the W. R. Grace mine employees had asbestosis. The mine was closed down, and Libby is now a *Superfund site*. The problem was not limited to Libby, however; 24 workers at the processing plant in Minneapolis have since died from asbestosis, and one resident who lived near the factory has also died.

Silica and Coal Dust

Other minerals can be hazardous if they are made into small airborne particles that can become lodged in the lungs. As with asbestos, both silica and coal mining operations release into the air large amounts of small dust particles, which are also known respectively as quartz dust and coal dust. Workers exposed to these types of dust are at risk for diseases that are broadly similar to asbestosis.

Trapper boy in West Virginia coal mine, 1908
(Library of Congress)

Quartz dust is commonly produced during rock drilling and sandblasting operations. These practices produce airborne particles of various sizes, the largest of which are naturally filtered by hair and mucous membranes during inhalation. However, some of the smallest particles can work their way deep into the lungs and get lodged in the air sacs, where they can do great harm. When small particles get trapped in the air sac, the lungs react by producing fibrolitic nodules and scar tissue around the trapped particles, reducing lung capacity in a disease called silicosis. This disease is easily preventable by simply wearing a respiratory mask when exposed to silica fibers, although this is not yet a common practice.

Coal dust has presented a long-term health problem in the United States and elsewhere in the world, with underground coal miners being at high risk for developing this disease. Mining operations inevitably release many fine particles of coal into the air. These particles also may get lodged in the lungs, resulting in a myriad of diseases including chronic bronchitis and emphysema, which are collectively known as black lung disease. The longer a miner works underground, the greater the risk of developing black lung disease. Miners who work underground for less than 10 years have about a 10 percent chance of developing these symptoms, whereas miners who have worked underground for more than 40 years have a 60 percent chance of developing black lung disease.

Lead

Lead is a metalliferous element used primarily for pipes, solder, batteries, bullets, pigments, radioactivity shields, and wheel weights. Lead is a known environmental hazard, and ingestion of large amounts of lead can lead to developmental problems in children, retardation, brain damage, and birth defects. It also may lead to kidney failure, multiple sclerosis, and brain cancer. Some researchers speculate that the fall of the Roman Empire was partly caused by lead poisoning. The Romans drank a lot of wine, and lead was concentrated at several different steps in the process they used to make the wine. The upper class also drank from lead cups and had water pumped into their homes in lead pipes. It is thought that lead poisoning contributed to brain damage, retardation, and the high incidence of birth defects among the Romans. These ideas are supported by the high contents of lead measured in the remains of some exhumed Roman burials. Remarkably, the lead content of ice cores from Greenland representing the Roman Empire period (500 B.C.E.–300 C.E.) also preserve about four times the normal level of lead, reflecting the increased mining and use of lead by the Romans.

Lead is present in the natural environment in several different forms. Galena is the most common ore mineral, forming shiny cubes with a silvery "lead" color. Lead is not generally hazardous in its natural mineral form, but becomes hazardous when mined and released from smelters as particulates, when leached from pipes or other fixtures, or when released into the air from automobile fumes. These processes can lead to high concentrations of native lead in soils, streams, and rivers. Lead may then be taken up by plants or aquatic organisms and thus enter the food chain where it can do great damage. Lead paint is also a great hazard in many homes in the United States, as lead was used as a paint additive until the 1970s. Paint in many older homes is peeling and ingested by infants, and paint along window frames is turned into airborne dust when windows are opened and closed. Environmental regulations in many states now require the removal of lead paint from homes upon the sale or leasing of properties.

The largest lead smelter in the United States, in Herculaneum, Missouri, is an example of the legacy of lead mining. Herculaneum is located about 30 miles south of St. Louis in the heart of the nation's largest lead deposit belt and has been the site of mining operations for generations. The problem in Herculaneum is that the town's smelter releases 34 tons of emissions per year (reduced from 800 tons per year a generation ago), including fine-grained lead dust. This rains down on the local community, and the local street dirt has been tested as containing 30 percent lead. Signs on the streets in town warn children not to play on the streets, curbs, or sidewalks, and parents are vigilant in attempting to keep the dust off toys, shoes, and out of the food and water supply. All their efforts have not been enough, though, and Missouri has replaced

NOT ALL CONCENTRATIONS OF MINERALS IN THE REGOLITH ARE HAZARDOUS: GOLD IN ALASKA

Although many concentrations of elements in the soil and regolith can pose significant risks to human health, some other concentrations of minerals present highly sought after economically valuable mineral deposits. The best example of this is the placer gold deposits of Alaska that lured tens of thousands of frontiersmen to the wild and dangerous territories of the north in the late 1800s and early 1900s. Life was extremely tough, the rewards few and dangers many, but some of these frontiersmen did find gold and managed to settle the north.

Gold typically occurs as a native metal and is found in lode deposits or placer deposits. Lode gold includes primary deposits in hard bedrock or in vein systems in the bedrock. In contrast, placer deposits are secondary, concentrated in stream gravels and soils. Gold is chemically unreactive so it persists through weathering and transportation and gets concentrated in soils and as heavy minerals in stream gravel deposits known as placers. Placer gold was the sought-after treasure in the great gold rushes of the Fairbanks gold district and the Yukon territories of Canada, where many placer and lode deposits are still being discovered and mined.

The placer gold mining in Alaska was really started after George Washington Carmack and his Native American brothers-in-law Skookum Jim and Tagish Charlie discovered rich deposits of placer gold on a tributary of the Klondike River in the Yukon Territory in 1896. Tens of thousands of would-be gold miners rushed to the Klondike in 1897–98, and many more struggled over the treacherous Chilkoot and White Passes in 1898, only to find that all of the streams and rivers in the area already had been claimed. Many of these entrepreneurs continued moving north into the wilderness of Alaska in their quest for gold. Alaska had only been purchased from Russia in 1867 and represented a new frontier. Gold had been reported from the Russian River on the Kenai Peninsula in 1834, and in 1886 the first major discovery of gold in interior Alaska was reported from the Fortymile River in interior Alaska. Other gold deposits were known from Birch Creek, in what is now the Circle Mining District.

The miners who left the Klondike district continued down the Yukon River to the coast on the Seward Peninsula and found gold on the beaches at Nome, starting a new gold rush to the coast. The beaches at Nome were also quickly staked and claimed, and many thousand of explorers and potential gold miners stopped between the Yukon and the beaches of Nome, searching for the precious metal in the soils and gravels of central Alaska. In 1902, Felix Pedro found gold along a tributary to the Tanana River, at the site of what is now the city of Fairbanks. This became the next gold rush area in Alaska and has led to many years of gold exploitation along the rivers and the establishment of what has become one of Alaska's biggest cities, founded on the concentration of gold in the regolith.

(continues)

(continued)

The early placer mining techniques were very labor intensive, with miners digging gravel from the streams, moving it in wheelbarrows, and washing it in sluices and gold pans in the search for the metal. Later, near the turn of the century, new techniques were developed where miners would build fires to melt the permafrost, tunnel to 20–30 feet (6–10 m) into the gravel and excavate huge piles that were later sluiced in the search for gold. Later techniques saw powerful firehoselike hydraulic nozzles used to thaw and loosen large quantities of gravel for sluicing. Then, in the 1930s, steam-powered shovels and bucketline dredges rapidly increased the pace of mining. Only in the 1980s did environmental concerns stop these methods of mining, where entire environments were stripped bare and barren gravels were laid back in the stream channel. Now, exploration for gold in the soils and regolith must be done under strict guidelines of the EPA.

the soil on 535 properties contaminated by lead. Many of the children and adults in the town are suffering the effects of lead poisoning, with retardation, stunted growth, hearing loss, and clusters of brain cancer and multiple sclerosis in town. One-quarter of all the children in the town tested positive for lead poisoning in 2001. Lead contamination has long been suspected in Herculaneum, but it wasn't until 2002 that the federal government stepped in. The EPA initiated (January 2002) a large-scale relocation program, initially moving 100 families with young children or pregnant women to safer locations. This may only be the beginning of the end, as former Congressman Dick Gephardt has suggested that the government shut down the Doe Run Lead Smelter and perhaps relocate the 2,800 families remaining in the town of Herculaneum. However, this mine and smelter, and others like it in South America, are still in operation in 2007.

Hazards of Radon Gas

Radon is a poisonous gas that is produced as a product of the radioactive decay product of the uranium decay series. Radon is a heavy gas, and it presents a serious indoor hazard in every part of the country. It tends to accumulate in poorly ventilated basements and well-insulated homes that are built on specific types of soil or bedrock that are rich in uranium minerals. Radon is known to cause lung cancer and, since it is an odorless, colorless gas, it can go unnoticed in homes for years. However, the hazard of radon is easily mitigated, and homes can be made safe once the hazard is identified.

Uranium is a radioactive mineral that spontaneously decays to lighter "daughter" elements by losing high-energy particles at a predictable rate known as a half-life. The half-life specifically measures how long it takes for half of the original or parent element to decay to the daughter element. Uranium decays to radium through a long series of steps with a cumulative half-life of 4.4 billion years. During these steps, intermediate daughter products are produced, and high-energy particles including alpha particles, consisting of two protons and two neutrons, are released. This produces heat. The daughter mineral radium is itself radioactive, and it decays with a half-life of 1,620 years by losing an alpha particle, thus forming the heavy gas radon. Since radon is a gas, it escapes out of the minerals and ground and makes its way to the atmosphere where it is dispersed, unless it gets trapped in people's homes. If it gets trapped, it can be inhaled and do damage. Radon is a radioactive gas, and it decays with a half-life of 3.8 days, producing daughter products of polonium, bismuth, and lead. If this decay occurs while the gas is in someone's lungs, then the solid daughter products become lodged in the lungs, which is how the damage from radon is initiated. Most of the

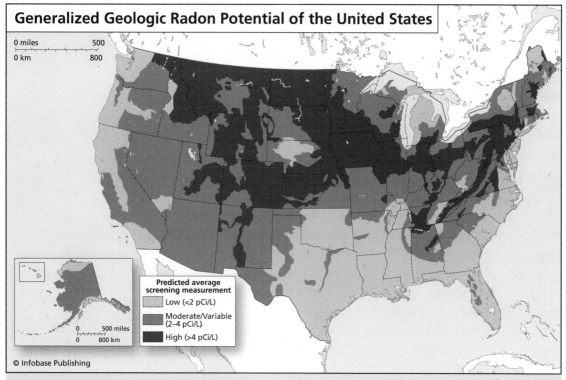

Map of radon gas hazards in the United States *(modeled after USGS)*

health risks from radon are associated with the daughter product polonium, which is easily lodged in lung tissue. Polonium is radioactive, and its decay and emission of high-energy particles in the lungs can damage lung tissue, eventually causing lung cancer.

There is a huge variation in the concentration of radon between geographic regions and in specific places in those regions. There is also a great variation in the concentration of the gas at different levels in the soil, home, and atmosphere. This variation is related to the concentration and type of radioactive elements present at a location. Radioactivity is measured in a unit known as a picocurie (pCi), which is approximately equal to the amount of radiation produced by the decay of two atoms per minute.

Soils have gases trapped between the individual grains that make up the soil, and these soil gases have typical radon levels of 20 pCi per liter to 100,000 pCi per liter, with most soils in the United States falling in the range of 200–2,000 pCi/L. Radon can also be dissolved in groundwater with typical levels falling between 100–2 million pCi/Liter. Outdoor air typically has 0.1–20 pCi/Liter, and radon inside people's homes ranges from 1–3,000 pCi/Liter, with 0.2 pCi/Liter being typical.

Why is there such a large variation in radon levels, and how can homeowners, water users, and others know which air is safe to breathe and which water is safe to drink? There are many natural geologic variations that lead to the complex distribution of hazardous radon, and these are examined below.

FORMATION AND MOVEMENT OF RADON GAS

One of the main variables controlling the concentration of radon at any site is the initial concentration of the parent element uranium in the underlying bedrock and soil. If the underlying materials have high concentrations of uranium, it is more likely that homes built in the area may have high concentrations of radon. Most natural geologic materials contain a small amount of uranium, typically about 1–3 parts per million (ppm). The concentration of uranium is typically about the same in soils derived from a rock as in the original source rock. However, some rock (and soil) types have much higher initial concentrations of uranium, ranging up to and above 100 ppm. Some of the rocks that have the highest uranium content include some granites, some types of volcanic rocks (especially the rhyolites), phosphate-bearing sedimentary rocks, and the metamorphosed equivalents of all of these rocks.

As the uranium in the soil gradually decays, it leaves its daughter product, radium, in concentrations proportional to the initial concentration of uranium. The radium then decays by forcefully ejecting an alpha particle from its nucleus. This ejection is an important step in the formation of radon, since every action has a reaction. In this case, the reaction is the recoil of the nucleus of the newly formed radon. Most radon remains trapped in minerals once it forms. However, if the decay of radium happens near the surface of a mineral, and if the recoil of the new nucleus of radon is away from the center of the grain, the radon gas may escape the bondage of the mineral. It will then be free to move in the intergranular space between minerals, soil, or cracks in the bedrock or become absorbed in groundwater between the mineral grains. Less than half (10–50 percent) of the radon produced by decay of radium actually escapes the host mineral. The rest is trapped inside where it eventually decays, leaving the solid daughter products behind as impurities in the mineral.

Once the radon is free in the open or water-filled pore spaces of the soil or bedrock, it may move rather quickly. The exact rate of movement is critical to whether or not the radon enters homes, because radon does not stay around for very long with a half-life of only 3.8 days. The rates at which radon moves through a typical soil depend on how much pore space there is in the soil (or rock), how connected these pore spaces are, and the exact geometry and size of the openings. Radon moves quickly through soils such as sand and gravel, with high *porosity* and *permeability.* However, it moves very slowly through less permeable materials such as clay. Radon also moves very quickly through fractured material, whether it is bedrock, clay, or concrete.

Considering how the rates of radon movement are influenced by the geometry of pore spaces in a soil or bedrock underlying a home, and how the initial concentration of uranium in the bedrock determines the amount of radon available to move, it becomes apparent that there should be a large variation in the concentration of radon from place to place. Homes built on dry permeable soils can accumulate radon quickly because it can migrate through the soil quickly. Conversely, homes built on impermeable soils and bedrock are unlikely to concentrate radon beyond their natural background levels.

Radon becomes hazardous when it enters homes and becomes trapped in poorly ventilated or well-insulated areas. Radon moves up through the soil and moves toward places with greater permeability. Home foundations are often built with a very porous and permeable

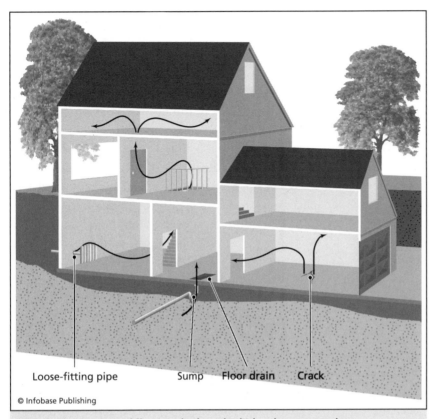

Loose-fitting pipe   Sump   Floor drain   Crack

© Infobase Publishing

Diagram showing many different paths through which radon can enter homes

gravel envelope surrounding the foundation to allow for water drainage. This also has the effect of focusing radon movement and bringing it close to the foundation, where the radon may enter through small cracks in the concrete, seams, spaces around pipes, sumps, and other openings, as well as through the concrete that may be moderately porous. Most modern homes intake less than 1 percent of their air from the soil. However, some homes, particularly older homes with cracked or poorly sealed foundations, low air pressure, and other entry points for radon, may intake as much as 20 percent of their internal air from the soil. These homes tend to have the highest concentrations of radon.

Radon can also enter the home and body through groundwater. Homes that rely on well water may be taking in water with high concentrations of dissolved radon. This radon can then be ingested or released from the water by agitation in the home. Radon is released by simple activities such as taking showers, washing dishes, or running faucets. Radon can also come from some municipal water supplies, such as those supplied by small towns that rely on well fields that take ground-water and distribute it to homes without providing a reservoir for the water to linger in while the radon decays to the atmosphere. Most larger cities, however, rely on reservoirs and surface water supplies, where the radon has had a chance to escape before being used by unsuspecting homeowners.

RADON HAZARD MAPPING

A greater understanding of the radon hazard risk in an area can be obtained through measuring and mapping the potential radon concentrations across that area. This can be done at many scales of observation. Radon concentrations can also be measured locally to know what kinds of mitigation are necessary to reduce the health risks posed by this poisonous gas.

The broadest sense of risk can be obtained by examining regional geologic maps and determining whether or not an area is located above potential high-uranium content rocks such as granites, shales, and rhyolites. These maps are available through the United States Geological Survey (USGS) and many state geological surveys. The U.S. Department of Energy has flown airplanes with radiation detectors across the country and produced maps that show the measured surface radioactivity on a regional scale. These maps give a very good indication of the amount of background uranium concentration in an area and thus are related to the potential risk for radon gas.

More detailed information is needed by local governments, businesses, and homeowners to assess whether or not they need to invest in radon remediation equipment. Geologists and environmental scientists are able to measure local soil radon gas levels using a variety of techniques, typically involving placing a pipe into the ground and sucking out the soil air for measurement. Other devices may be buried in the soil to more passively measure the formation of the damage produced by alpha particle emission. Using such information, the radon concentrations in certain soil types can be established. This information can be integrated with soil characteristic maps produced by the U.S. Department of Agriculture (USDA) and by state and county officials to make more regional maps of potential radon hazards and risks.

Most homeowners must resort to private measurements of radon concentrations in their homes by using commercial devices that detect radon or measure the damage from alpha particle emission. The measurement of radon levels in homes has become a standard part of home sales transactions, so more data and awareness of the problem has risen in the past 10 years. The remediation of radon problems in homes or businesses has become relatively simple. An engineer or contractor can be hired simply and cheaply (typically less than $1,000 for an average home) to design and build a ventilation system that can remove the harmful radon gas, making the air safe to breathe.

Conclusion

The formation of regolith and soil involves the breakdown of solid rock and the removal of the dissolvable component of the rocks, leaving the residual material behind in the soil. This process concentrates certain elements, and some of these can be harmful to human health. Some of the most hazardous elements that are common in soils include selenium, arsenic, radon, and lead, while mines may expose workers to other harmful elements such as coal dust, silica dust, and asbestos fibers. A variety of health conditions and ailments around the world, generally in the poorer populations, are caused by exposure or ingestion of hazardous elements in the soil. Careful monitoring of the concentrations of these elements in developed nations such as the United States has greatly reduced the health threat from these elements.

3

Water in the Regolith: Expansive Clays, Liquefaction, and Groundwater Pollution

Under certain conditions some types of soil can prove to be physically hazardous. There are many different types of soils, and most of them are relatively inert. However, other soils expand and contract dramatically with changes in seasonal moisture content, causing damage to structures built on them. Other soils become soft and liquidlike quicksand when agitated and may swallow people and structures. Still other soils contain high concentrations of contaminated water, organic material that can burn for years, radioactive gases, and other elements that can prove hazardous. In this chapter, hazardous physical aspects of soil geology are discussed. This includes how the material properties of soils can change with the addition of water and groundwater pollution.

Physical Properties of Soil

Soil can be defined as that part of the regolith that can support rooted plants. Soil is formed by a combination of physical and chemical weathering and by organic decay. The organic component is important, because organic decay produces nutrients to support plant life. Soils are complex ecosystems, and every cubic yard may contain millions of living organisms. Soils are important parts of the environment and determine land use patterns, the types of agriculture that can be supported, which areas have groundwater *aquifers,* and which are aquicludes that stop the movement of water. Soils also play a vital role in locating sites of waste disposal, buildings, and other structures. The material properties of soils are very variable and are determined by the constituents and control hillslope stability, landslide potential, and groundshaking potential during earthquakes. Water in the pore spaces of regolith may exert significant pressure on surrounding materials and decrease the frictional resistance of one block on top of another, as explained in the sidebar on page 33 on the Hubbert and Rubey beer can experiment.

The amount of water saturation in soils is extremely variable both from place to place and in time at any given place. Water saturation of soils is important for understanding soil hazards, since water saturation largely controls the mechanical properties of soils. The influence of water on the mechanical properties of soil can be appreciated by considering attempts to build two sandcastles: one in dry sand and one in wet sand. Both sands may be exactly the same in all aspects except for water content. Attempts to build sandcastles in the wet sand are successful—the sand sticks together and walls, towers, and tunnels can be constructed. However, attempts to build sandcastles in dry sand will be unfruitful. Walls will slide and remain at the *angle of repose* (an unsatisfactory 22 degrees for sandcastles), towers cannot be constructed, and tunnels are hopeless. The simple addition of water changes the mechanical properties so much that the castle can be constructed.

The effect of water may be the opposite in soils with different structures, particularly those with more clay minerals. This is exemplified by clay-rich road surfaces that are common in many desert environments. When these are dry, driving on them is simple and stable, though dusty. However, if it rains the clay becomes wet and slippery, and the road may become nearly impossible to drive on. Likewise, water in many soils percolates through the pores and lubricates grain boundaries, making the entire soil unstable.

Engineers determine the potential hazards of soils by evaluating several different properties of the soil. The most significant variables are the size of the particles in the soil, the types of solid particles, and how much water is present. Porosity and permeability are important, as is the overall mixture of solid, liquid, and gas.

The strength of a soil is a function of frictional forces, determined by the soil's particle size, shape, density, surface roughness, and several other factors. A soil's cohesion, or how well the particles stick together, is a function of the water content of the soil as well as the strength of the molecular and electrostatic forces.

The *sensitivity* of a soil is a measure of how the strength changes with shaking or with other disturbances such as those associated with excavation or construction. Sensitivity is dependent on soil type and particularly on clay content. Soils with high clay contents may lose up to 75 percent of their strength with shaking, whereas sand- and gravel-rich soils tend to be less sensitive and retain more of their strength during shaking.

The compressibility of a soil is determined by many things, foremost of which is the amount of fine-grained and organic materials present in it. Many of these materials are prone to settling when they are built on.

The *corrosiveness* of a soil is a measure of its ability to corrode or chemically decompose buried objects, such as pipes, wires, tanks, and posts. The composition of the soil and the composition of the buried material, as well as the amount of water percolating through the soil, determine a soil's corrosiveness.

The *shrink/swell potential* of a soil is extremely important to know for construction to begin in an area. The shrink/swell potential is a measure of a soil's ability to add or lose water at a molecular level. Some particular types of clays are said to be *expansive soils,* and they add layers of water molecules between the plates of clay minerals (made of silica, aluminum, and oxygen), loosely bonding the water in the mineral structure. Damage from shrinking and swelling clays in soils is the most costly of all natural hazards and disasters, costing more than $2 billion a year in the United States alone. Most expansive clays are rich in montmorillonite, a clay mineral that can expand up to 15 times its normal dry size. Most soils do not expand more than 25–50 percent above their dry volume, but it must be remembered that an expansion of 3 percent is considered hazardous.

Damage from shrinking/swelling soils is mostly to bridges, foundations, and roadways, all of which may crack and move during expansion. Regions with pronounced wet and dry seasons tend to have a greater problem with expansive clays than regions with more uniform precipitation distributed throughout the year. This is because the changes in the adhered water content of the clays changes less in regions where the soil moisture remains more constant. Some damage from shrinking and swelling soils can be limited, especially around homes. Trees that are growing near foundations can cause soil shrinkage during dry seasons and expansion in wet seasons. These dangers of shrinking/swelling soils can be avoided by not planting trees too closely to homes and other structures. Local topography and drainage details also influence the site-specific shrink/swell potential. Buildings should not be placed in areas with poor drainage as water may accumulate and lead to increased soil expansion. Local drainage may be modified to allow runoff away from building sites, reducing the hazards associated with soil expansion.

In general, soils that are rich in clay minerals and organic material tend to have low strength, low permeability, high compressibility, and the greatest shrink/swell potential. These types of soils should be avoided for construction projects when possible. If they cannot be avoided, steps must be taken to accommodate these undesirable traits into the building construction. Sand- and gravel-rich soils pose much less danger than clay and organic rich soils. These soils are well drained and strong, have low compressibility and sensitivity, and have low shrink/swell potential.

Cracked wall due to expansive soil *(USGS)*

Quicksand and Soil Liquefaction

Some types of soils turn into unstable quicksandlike masses when they are shaken by earthquakes or other earth tremors. *Liquefaction* is a process where sudden shaking of certain types of water-saturated sands and muds turns these once-solid sediments into a slurry, a sediment/water mixture, with a liquidlike consistency. Liquefaction occurs through a process where the shaking causes individual grains to move apart and water moves in between the individual grains making the whole water/sediment mixture behave like a fluid. Earthquakes often cause liquefaction of sands and muds, and any structures that are built on sediments that liquefy may suddenly sink into them as if they were resting on a thick fluid. Liquefaction also causes sand to bubble to the surface during earthquakes, forming mounds up to several tens of feet high known as sand volcanoes, or ridges of sand. Liquefaction is also responsible for the sinking of sidewalks, telephone poles, building foundations, and other structures during earthquakes.

Liquefaction is responsible for a large amount of damage in some earthquakes, such as the Kobe, Japan, earthquake of 1995, the Loma Prieta earthquake in California in 1989, and the Alaskan earthquake of 1964. One famous example of liquefaction occurred in the 1964 Niigata, Japan, earthquake, where entire rows of apartment buildings rolled onto their sides, but were not severely damaged internally.

THE ROLE OF WATER AS A LUBRICANT TO INITIATE MASS WASTING: INSIGHTS FROM THE HUBBERT AND RUBEY BEER CAN EXPERIMENT

"Mass wasting" is defined as the downslope movement of regolith without the direct aid of water, yet it is clear that water is often involved in various ways in downslope flows and landslides. First, water is mixed with many of the soils, rocks, and other material that slide or fall downhill during mass wasting events, and many landslides and debris flows occur immediately after or during periods of exceptionally high rainfall. In some cases, water helps the sediments become more liquid so that they flow more easily, especially in the more fluid types of flows such as *mudflows* and debris flows.

Water may play a more significant role in initiating rock and debris falls, avalanches, and slides. Common experience reveals that wet surfaces have less frictional resistance than dry surfaces. Cars skid off wet roads more easily than dry, and people slip on wet floors more often than on dry ones. The same is true for rocks and regolith surfaces that are on the verge of slipping. In dry times, the contact surfaces between surfaces that might later slip are marked by contacts between hard and dry grains of rock or soil, and dry contacts tend to have higher frictional resistance than wet surfaces. If water from heavy rainfalls, snowmelt, or other sources can penetrate rocks and infiltrate along potential slip surfaces, then the frictional resistance is dramatically reduced. In some cases, this reduction in friction is enough to make the rock or regolith mass slip, and a landslide results.

This effect is illustrated by the "Hubbert and Rubey Beer Can Experiment" first described in a paper published in 1959 in the *Bulletin of the Geological Society of America*. Although their experiment was initially designed to explain the effects of fluid pressure in allowing large, low-angle faults to move, the basic principles are relevant for mass wasting. The experiment can be performed as follows: Take a smooth planar surface of glass and set up a slight incline of about 1 percent. Remove the lid of a beer (or other appropriate beverage) can, empty its contents, and ensure that the cut edge (with the hole) is smooth and even. Chill the empty beer can in a freezer. Then, wet the surface of the glass plate and place the cold beer can upside down on the plate. As the can warms, the air inside expands, increasing the fluid pressure across the plate/can contact, and the can starts to slide down the gentle slope. It continues to slide until the lip of the can passes over the edge of the glass plate, releasing the air in the can. If the experiment is performed again on a dry plate, the can does not move.

The beer can experiment illustrates that high fluid pressures along contacts between bedrock (modeled as the glass plate) and overburden of regolith (the beer can) can effectively reduce the friction along the contact and allow the overburden to slide down even very gentle slopes. Water from rain can seep into cracks, joints, or spaces between grains and reduce the friction along contacts. In this way, water can lubricate surfaces and promote landslide formation during periods of heavy rainfall.

Groundwater Contamination

Freshwater is one of the most important resources in the world. Wars have been and will be fought over the ability to obtain freshwater, and water rights are hot political issues in places where it is scarce, like the American West and the Middle East. Since we live in a world with a finite amount of freshwater and since the global population is growing so rapidly, it is likely that freshwater will become an increasingly important topic for generations to come.

The upper layers of the soil and regolith are in many places saturated with water. This water is responsible for the mechanical behavior of the soil and also is important in its own right as a resource. Less than 1 percent of the planet's water is groundwater, which may be defined as all the water contained within spaces in bedrock, soil, and regolith. However, the volume of groundwater is 35 times the volume of freshwater in lakes and streams. All over the world, people are realizing that groundwater is a vital resource for their nation's survival and are beginning to appreciate how much of the world's groundwater resources have become contaminated by natural and human-aided processes. Approximately 40 percent of drinking water in the United States comes from groundwater reservoirs. About 80 billion gallons (302.8 l) of groundwater are pumped out of these reservoirs every day in the United States.

Where does this water come from? It comes from rainfall that seeps into the ground and slowly makes its way downhill toward the sea. There is water everywhere beneath the ground, mostly within 2,500 feet (750 m) of the surface. The volume of groundwater is estimated to be equivalent to a layer that is 180 feet (55 m) thick and is spread evenly over the Earth's land surface.

The distribution of water in the ground can be divided into the unsaturated and the saturated zones. The top of the water table is defined as the upper surface of the saturated zone. Below this surface, all openings are filled with water.

THE GROUNDWATER SYSTEM

Groundwater is best thought of as a system of many different parts. Some of these act as conduits and reservoirs and others as off-ramps and on-ramps into the groundwater system. Recharge areas are where water enters the groundwater system, and discharge areas are where water leaves the groundwater system. In humid climates, recharge areas encompass nearly the land's entire surface except for streams and floodplains, whereas in desert climates, recharge areas consist mostly of the mountains and alluvial fans. Discharge areas consist mostly of streams and lakes.

The level of the water table changes with the amount of precipitation. In humid regions, it reflects the topographic variation, whereas in dry times or places it tends to flatten out to the level of the streams or lakes. Water flows faster when the slope is greatest, so groundwater flows faster during wet times. The fastest rate of groundwater flow yet observed in the United States is 800 feet per year (250 m/year).

Aquifers include any body of permeable rock or regolith saturated with water through which groundwater moves. Gravels and sandstone make good aquifers, but clay is so impermeable that it makes bad aquifers or even aquicludes. Other fractured rock bodies also make good aquifers.

Springs are places where groundwater flows out at the ground surface. Springs can form where the ground surface intersects the water table or at a vertical or horizontal change in permeability, such as where water in gravels on a hillslope overlays a clay unit, and the water flows out on the hill along the gravel/clay boundary.

Most wells fill with water simply because they intersect the water table. However, the rocks below the surface are not always homogeneous, which can result in a complex type of water table known as a perched water table. These can result from discontinuous bodies in the subsurface, which create bodies of water at elevations higher than the main water table.

In many regions, a permeable layer, typically a sandstone, is confined between two impermeable beds, creating a confined aquifer. In these systems, water only enters the system in a small recharge area and, if this is in the mountains, then the aquifer may be under considerable pressure. This is known as an *artesian system.* Water that escapes the system from the fracture or well reflects the pressure difference between the elevation of the source area and the discharge area (hydraulic gradient), and it rises above the aquifer as an artesian spring or artesian well. Some of these wells have made fountains that have spewed water 200 feet (60 m) high. One example of an artesian system is found in Florida, where water enters the recharge area and is released near Miami about 19,000 years later.

Groundwater also reacts chemically with the surrounding rocks; it may deposit minerals and cement together grains, causing a reduction in porosity and permeability, or form features like stalactites and stalagmites in caves. In other cases, particularly when water moves through limestone, it may dissolve the rock, forming caves and underground tunnels. Where these dissolution cavities intersect the surface of the Earth, they form *sinkholes.*

MOVEMENT OF GROUNDWATER

Most of the water under the ground doesn't just sit there; it is constantly in motion, although rates are typically only 1–2 inches (2–5 cm) per day. The rates of movement are controlled by the amount of open space in the bedrock or regolith and how the spaces are connected.

Porosity is the percentage of total volume of a body that consists of open spaces. Sands and gravels typically have about 20 percent open spaces, whereas clays have about 50 percent. The sizes and shapes of grains determine their porosity, which is also influenced by how much they are compacted, cemented together, or deformed.

In contrast, permeability is a body's capacity to transmit fluids or to allow fluids to move through its open pore spaces. Permeability is not directly related to porosity, because if all the pore spaces in a body are isolated, then it may have high porosity, but the water may be trapped and unable to move through the body. Permeability is also affected by molecular attraction, the force that makes thin films of water stick to things instead of being forced to the ground by gravity. If the pore spaces in a material are very small, as in a clay, then the force of molecular attraction is strong enough to stop the water from flowing through the body. When the pores are large, the water in the center of the pores is free to move.

After a rainfall, much of the water stays near the surface, because clay in the near-surface horizons of the soil retains much water because of its molecular attraction. This forms a layer of soil moisture in many regions and is able to sustain seasonal plant growth.

Some of this near-surface water evaporates, and some is used by plants. Other water runs directly off into streams. The remaining water seeps into the saturated zone or into the water table. Once in the saturated zone it moves by percolation, gradually and slowly, from high areas to low areas under the influence of gravity. These lowest areas are usually lakes or streams. Many streams form where the water table intersects the surface of the land.

Once in the water table, the paths that individual particles follow vary and the transit time from surface to stream may vary from days to thousands of years along a single hillside. Water can flow upward because of high pressure at depth and low pressure in streams.

HAZARDOUS ELEMENTS IN GROUNDWATER

Natural groundwater is typically rich in dissolved elements and compounds derived from the soil, regolith, and bedrock that the water has migrated through. Some of these dissolved elements and compounds are poisonous, whereas others are tolerable in small concentrations but harmful in high concentrations. Groundwater is also increasingly becoming contaminated by human and industrial waste, and the overuse of groundwater resources has caused groundwater levels to drop and led to other problems, especially along coastlines. Seawater may move in to replace depleted freshwater, and the ground surface may subside when the water is removed from the pore spaces in aquifers.

The U.S. Public Health Service has established limits on the concentrations of dissolved substances (called total dissolved solids, or TDS) in natural water that is used for domestic and other uses. The table below lists these standards for the United States. It should be emphasized that many other countries, particularly those with chronic water shortages, have much more lenient standards. Sweet water, free of excessive acidity, is preferred for domestic use and has less than 500 milligrams of total dissolved solids per liter of water. Fresh and slightly saline water, with TDS of 1,000–3,000 mg/L, is suitable for use by livestock and for irrigation. Water with higher concentrations of TDS is unfit for humans or livestock. Irrigation of fields using waters with high concentrations of TDS is also not recommended as the water will evaporate and leave the

Standards for Total Dissolved Solids in Drinking Water	
WATER CLASSIFICATION	TOTAL DISSOLVED SOLIDS (TDS)
Sweet	< 500 mg/L
Fresh	500–1,000 mg/L
Slightly saline	1,000–3,000 mg/L
Moderately saline	3,000–10,000 mg/L
Very saline	10,000–35,000 mg/L
Brine	> 35,000 mg/L

dissolved salts and minerals behind, degrading and eventually destroying the productivity of the land.

The quality of groundwater can be reduced or considered contaminated by either a high amount of TDS or by the introduction of a specific toxic element. Most of the TDS in groundwaters are salts that have been derived from dissolution of the local bedrock or from soils derived from the bedrock. Salts may also seep into groundwater from the sea along coastlines, particularly if the water is being pumped out for use. In these cases, seawater often moves in to replace the depleted freshwater.

Dissolved salts in groundwater commonly include the bicarbonate (HCO_3) and sulfate (SO_4) ions, which are often attached to other ions. Dissolved calcium (Ca) and magnesium (Mg) ions can cause water to become hard. "Hard water" is defined as containing more than 120 parts per million of dissolved calcium and magnesium. Hard water is difficult to lather with soap, and it forms a crusty mineralization buildup on faucets and pipes. Adding sodium (Na) in a water softener can soften hard water, but people with heart problems or those on a low-salt diet should not do this. Hard water is common in areas where the groundwater has moved through limestone or dolostone rocks, which contain high concentrations of calcium and magnesium that are easily dissolved by groundwater.

Groundwater may have many other contaminants, some natural and others that are the result of human activity. Natural contaminants include the group of elements previously described (selenium, arsenic, etc.); human pollutants, including animal and human waste, pesticides, industrial solvents, petroleum products, and other chemicals, are also a serious problem in many areas.

Groundwater contamination, whether natural or human-induced, is a serious problem because of the importance of the limited water supply. Pollutants in the groundwater system do not simply wash away with the next rain, as many dissolved toxins in the surface water system do. Groundwater pollutants typically have a residence time, or average length of time they remain in the system, of hundreds or thousands of years. Many groundwater systems are capable of cleaning themselves of natural biological contaminants using bacteria, but chemical contaminants have longer residence times.

ARSENIC IN GROUNDWATER

Arsenic poisoning leads to a variety of horrific diseases, including hyperpigmentation (abundance of red freckles), hyperkeratosis (scaly lesions on the skin), cancerous lesions on the skin, and squamous cell carcinoma (a type of skin cancer). Arsenic may be introduced into the food chain and body in several ways. In Guizhou Province, China, villagers dry their chili peppers indoors over coal fires. Unfortunately, the coal is rich in arsenic (containing up to 35,000 parts per million arsenic), and much of this arsenic is transferred to the chili peppers during the drying process. Thousands of the local villagers are now suffering arsenic poisoning, with cancers and other diseases ruining families and entire villages.

Most naturally occurring arsenic is introduced into the food chain through drinking contaminated groundwater. Arsenic in groundwater is commonly formed by the dissolution of minerals from weathered rocks and soils. In Bangladesh and West Bengal, India, 25–75 million people are at risk for arsenosis because of high concentrations of natural arsenic in groundwater.

In 1975, the maximum allowable level of arsenic in drinking water in the United States was set at 50 parts per billion. The EPA adopted new standards on the allowable levels of arsenic in drinking water that went into effect on January 23, 2006. Following recommendations of scientists from the National Academy of Sciences (NAS), the allowable levels of arsenic were lowered to 10 parts per billion, providing better protection for approximately 13 million Americans who were drinking water with higher arsenic concentrations prior to 2006.

Arsenic is not concentrated evenly in groundwater. The USGS issued a series of maps in 2000 showing the concentration of arsenic in tens of thousands of groundwater wells in the United States. Arsenic is concentrated mostly in the southwestern part of the United States, with a few peaks elsewhere such as southern Texas, parts of Montana (due to mining operations), and parts of the upper Plains. Perhaps a remediation plan that attacks the highest concentrations of arsenic would be the most cost effective with the highest health benefit.

CONTAMINATION BY SEWAGE

A major problem of groundwater contamination is sewage. If coliform bacteria get into the groundwater, the aquifer is ruined, and care must be taken and samples analyzed before the water is used for drinking. In many cases, sand filtering can remove bacteria, and aquifers contaminated by coliform bacteria and other human waste can be cleaned more easily than aquifers contaminated by many other elemental and mineral toxins.

Although serious, detailed discussion of groundwater contamination by human waste is beyond the scope of this book. The reader is referred to the sources listed at the end of the chapter for more detailed accounts.

Hazards of Natural (and Induced) Underground Fires

In many places around the world, fires have been burning in underground deposits of coal and other flammable rock material for hundreds or even thousands of years. Fires in underground coal seams have been ignited by lightning, surface fires, and spontaneous combustion for millions of years. These fires scorch the overlying surface material, turning it into a barren brittle material known as clinker. Recently, the incidence of fires has increased dramatically because of mining operations and other human activities. Thousands of underground fires are currently burning on the planet, with most concentrated in Asia, where it is estimated that approximately 20 percent of China's annual coal production is burned in underground fires.

Underground fires present numerous hazards. First, they release poisonous gases through cracks, fissures, and other openings to the surface. These fumes kill vegetation and pollute the air and are contributing a large volume of greenhouse gases to the atmosphere, thus contributing to global warming. It is estimated that millions of tons of carbon dioxide alone are being added to the atmosphere by underground fires. The volume of carbon dioxide produced annually by underground coal fires in China is approximately equal to that produced by all the cars and small trucks in the United States.

Once the underground fires burn through an area, the coal seam is gone and leaves an unsupported roof over the former seam. This causes instability, and the roof may collapse into the space formerly occupied by the coal seam. Such collapse often extends to the surface, where sinkholes and other collapse structures may swallow formerly productive land. In cases where the fires are burning closer to the surface, *subsidence* may occur as the fire burns, turning the land into a sunken moonscape of clinker.

Ignition of underground fires may occur several different ways. First, if a flammable rock such as coal is exposed at the surface, it may be ignited by surface fires or lightning. As the fire burns, it can spread underground and burn for tens, hundreds, or thousands of years until the fuel is used up. One underground coal fire in Australia, known as Burning Mountain, has been burning for at least 2,000 years. Fires can

Vent for underground fire burning in Centralia, Pennsylvania *(Corbis)*

also ignite spontaneously. Minerals in the coal such as pyrite release small amounts of heat when they are exposed to oxygen. If the coal is in an enclosed area, such as a mine or natural cavity, then the heat can build up and eventually ignite the coal. Underground coal and peat can also ignite from forest fires or lightning strikes, such as those that plagued the Indonesian region in 1997 after years of drought. Smoke from the Indonesian fires and burning underground fuel made its way thousands of miles across the ocean to Australia and the Pacific island regions. Underground fires sparked by surface fires in Indonesia are burning to this day.

Humans have ignited other underground fires. For instance, an underground fire in a coal seam in Centralia, Pennsylvania, has been burning since 1961 and has destroyed much of the town over the path of the fire. The fire was ignited when trash dumped into an abandoned mine shaft caught fire and ignited the coal seam exposed on the mine wall. The fire spread through the existing tunnels that provided the perfect mix of fuel, air, and heat. As the fire moves through the tunnels and outward along the coal seam, the overlying land smolders and turns into clinker. The U.S. government has had to buy out and evict most of Centralia's residents, at a cost of $40 million to taxpayers.

It is extremely difficult to extinguish underground fires. Several methods have been tried with limited success. First, barriers can be constructed in tunnels to attempt to block the movement of the fire, but in many cases the fires can burn right around the barriers. Tunnels can be filled with solid or foam material, but if the fire has moved away from the tunnels into the coal seam, this will also be ineffective. Noncombustible gases can be pumped into the caves or mines to suffocate the fire by depriving it of fuel. This is also difficult, as many of the mines are very porous, and the noncombustible gases can escape outward while oxygen can move inward. In a few examples, the surface area over burning underground fires has been dammed and flooded, causing water to seep into the ground and extinguish the fires. However, in most cases, underground fires continue to burn, and nearby residents must adapt to the situation. Many coal seams in China and India are actively mined as they burn, and residents live nearby breathing the toxic fumes.

Living next to burning underground coal fires is extremely hazardous, as demonstrated by the Jharia mine in India, which has been on fire since 1916. This long-burning fire caused a mine wall to collapse in 1995, releasing surface water into the mine. The sudden influx of water caused a steam explosion, killing 60 miners. This disaster did not hinder further operations in the mine, however. The population around the mines has more than doubled in the past 20 years, putting even more people at risk.

Conclusion

Clay minerals and other components of soil have variable mechanical properties that change the behavior of different types of soils under different conditions. Some soils dramatically expand or contract in volume with the addition or subtraction of water. The expansive soils cause large amounts of damage to structures by cracking foundations, walls, bridges, and other things, causing billions of dollars of damage in the United States alone every year. Other soils may behave like a liquid when shaken during earthquakes, causing structures to collapse.

Groundwater can also move through soils and may become contaminated with harmful natural elements or human pollution, becoming dangerous to use as drinking water. Some of the most hazardous elements that are common in soils and in groundwater include selenium, arsenic, radon, and lead. A variety of health conditions and ailments around the world, generally in the poorer populations, are caused by exposure or ingestion of hazardous elements in the soil and the groundwater systems. Careful monitoring of the concentrations of these elements in developed nations such as the United States has greatly reduced the health threat from these elements.

Underground fires represent a significant hazard to global climate, as the carbon dioxide released from underground coal fires in China alone is approximately equal to the amount of carbon dioxide released by all automobiles in the United States. Underground fires also pose local hazards to air quality, cause surface collapse, and can initiate steam explosions if the fires encounter groundwater reservoirs.

4

Mass Wasting Processes

Mass wasting is the movement of soil, regolith, or rock downhill without the direct aid of water. The movement may be slow, even imperceptible, as in the case of *creep*, or may be sudden and involve huge volumes of material, as in *debris avalanches.* Gravity is the main driving force behind mass wasting processes, as it is constantly pulling on material and attempting to force it downhill. This is because, on a slope, gravity can be resolved into two components, one perpendicular to the slope and one parallel to the slope. The steeper the angle of the slope, the greater the influence of gravity. The effect of gravity reaches a maximum along vertical or overhanging cliffs.

The tangential component of gravity tends to pull material downhill and results in mass wasting. When the tangential component of gravity (gt on figure) is great enough to overcome the force of friction at the base of the boulder, the boulder falls downhill, resulting in a mass wasting event. The friction is really a measure of the resistance to gravity—the greater the friction, the greater the resistance to gravity's pull. Friction can be greatly reduced by lubrication of surfaces in contact, allowing the two materials to slide past one another more easily. Water is a common lubricating agent, so mass wasting events tend to occur more frequently during times of heavy or prolonged rain. For a mass wasting event or a mass movement to occur, the lubricating forces must be strong enough to overcome the resisting forces that tend to hold the boulder in place against the force of gravity. Lubricating forces include the cohesion between similar particles (like one clay molecule

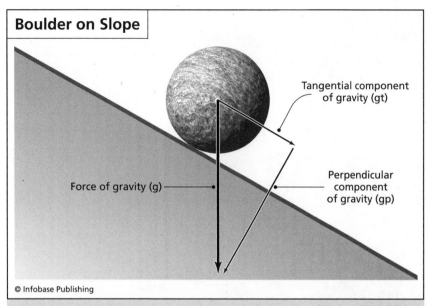

Boulder on Slope

Tangential component of gravity (gt)

Perpendicular component of gravity (gp)

Force of gravity (g)

© Infobase Publishing

Force diagram for mass wasting. Gravity acting on a boulder on a slope can be broken into two components, one parallel to the slope (gt) and one perpendicular to the slope (gp).

to another) and the adhesion between different or unlike particles (like the boulder to the clay beneath it). When the resisting forces are greater than the driving force (tangential component of gravity), the slope is steady and the boulder stays in place. When lubricating components reduce the resisting forces so much that the driving forces are greater than the resisting forces, slope failure occurs.

The process of the movement of regolith downslope (or underwater) may occur rapidly or it may proceed slowly. In any case, slopes on mountainsides typically evolve toward steady state angles known as the angle of repose balanced by material moving in from upslope and out from downslope. This angle of repose is also a function of the grain size of the regolith.

Driving forces for mass wasting can also be increased by human activity. Excavation for buildings, roads, or other features along the lower portions of slopes may actually remove parts of the slopes, causing them to become steeper than they were before construction and to exceed the angle of repose. This will cause the slopes to become unstable or metastable and susceptible to collapse. Building structures on the tops of slopes will also make them unstable, as the extra weight of the building adds extra stresses to the slope that may be enough to initiate the collapse of the slope.

Photo of base of slope scree deposit that shows large angular boulders that fell from cliff in background. Alpine, New Jersey *(Photo Researchers, Inc.)*

Weathered rock debris accumulates at the bases of mountain slopes, deposited there by *rockfalls*, slides, and other downslope movements. The entire body of rock waste sloping away from the mountains is known as talus, and the sediment composing it is known as sliderock. Sliderock tends to accumulate at the angle of repose, which depends on the way the particles are packed together, their shapes and sizes. Most angles of repose slopes form at 33–37 degrees.

Physical Conditions That Control Mass Wasting

Whether or not mass wasting occurs and its type is controlled by many factors. These include characteristics of the regolith and bedrock, the presence or absence of water, overburden, angle of the slope, and the way that the particles are packed together.

Mass wasting in solid bedrock terrain is strongly influenced by pre-existing weaknesses in the rock that make movement along them easier than if the weaknesses were not present. For instance, bedding planes, joints, and fractures, if favorably oriented, may act as planes of weakness along which giant slabs of rock may slide downslope. If the rock or regolith has many pores, or open spaces between grains, it will be weaker than a rock without pores. This is because there is no material in the pores. If the open spaces were filled, the material in the pore space could hold the rock together. Furthermore, pore spaces allow fluids to pass through the rock or regolith, and the fluids may further dissolve the rock, creating more pore space and further weakening the material. Water in open pore spaces may also exert pressure on the surrounding rocks, pushing individual grains apart and making the rock weaker.

Water may act to either enhance or inhibit movement of regolith and rock downhill. Water inhibits downslope movement when the pore spaces are only partly filled with water and the surface tension (bonding of water molecules along the surface) acts as an additional force holding grains together. This surface tension is able to bond water grains to each other, water grains to rock particles, and rock particles to each other. An everyday example of how effective surface tension may be at holding particles together is found in paper sticking to glass. A dry sheet of paper will slide off a window, but adheres to the window if it is wet. However, if too much water is added the paper will slide off the window to the ground.

Water more typically acts to reduce the adhesion between grains, promoting downslope movements. When the pore spaces are filled, the water acts as a lubricant and may actually exert forces that push individual grains apart. The weight of the water in pore spaces also exerts additional pressure on underlying rocks and soils, and this is known as loading. The loading from water in pore spaces is in many cases enough so that the strength of the underlying rocks and soil is exceeded and the slope fails, resulting in a downslope movement.

Another important effect of water in pore spaces occurs when the water freezes. When water freezes, it expands by a few percent, and this expansion exerts enormous pressures on surrounding rocks, in many cases pushing them apart. The freeze-thaw cycles found in many climates are responsible for many of the downslope movements in these regions.

Steep slopes are less stable than shallow slopes. Loose unconsolidated material tends to form slopes at specific angles that, depending on the specific characteristics of the material, range from about 33–37 degrees. The way that the particles are arranged or packed in the slope is also a factor, and the denser the packing, the more stable the slope.

Initiation of Mass Wasting

Earthquakes or long periods of rain typically trigger landslides and other mass wasting events. Earthquakes may cause prolonged shaking of the ground, loosening boulders, starting avalanches, *slumps*, and

Photograph of eroding coastal cliff in Norfolk, England (*Associated Press*)

other *downslope flows.* Earthquake-induced landslides occur in areas with steep slopes or cliffs. One of the worst recorded earthquake-induced landslides occurred in the 1970 magnitude 7.8 earthquake in Peru, in which at least 18,000 people were killed.

When highways are built through mountains, slopes may be modified, so that the new slope exceeds the angle of repose. This is just asking for trouble. Retaining walls can delay catastrophic failure, but rarely prevent it. Many new technologies are being developed to improve the record of retaining walls and overall mitigation of landslide hazards. These techniques are discussed in chapter 7.

Along many shorelines with cliffs, the top of the cliff juts out over the water and the base of the cliff is eroded more deeply back into the land. Cliffs with this shape are referred to as undercut. Streams and ocean waves often undercut waterside cliffs, making them very unstable, especially during storms when waves bash against the cliffs. The undercutting increases erosion from the top of the cliff, as the slope tries to regain its angle of repose. In other cases, the slope may suddenly and catastrophically fail in a slump or slide. In many cases the cliffs fail during or soon after storms, so it is advisable to stay away from cliffs after storms.

Shaking and slope oversteepening associated with volcanic eruptions typically trigger large numbers of mass wasting events. If ice and glaciers lie on the volcano, they can melt and trigger more mass wasting.

Types of Mass Wasting

Mass movements are of three basic types, distinguished by the way the rock, soil, water, and debris move. *Slides* move over and in contact with the underlying surface. *Flows* include movements of regolith, rock, water, and air in which the moving mass breaks into many pieces that flow in a chaotic mass movement. *Falls* move freely through the air and land at the base of the slope or escarpment. There is a continuity between different processes of mass wasting, but many differ in terms of the velocity of downslope movement and the relative concentrations of sediment, water, and air. A landslide is a general name for any downslope movement of a mass of bedrock, regolith, or a mixture of rock and soil, and it is used here to indicate any mass wasting process. Since all mass wasting processes occur on slopes, the most common types of events are discussed first, beginning with the failure of a slope.

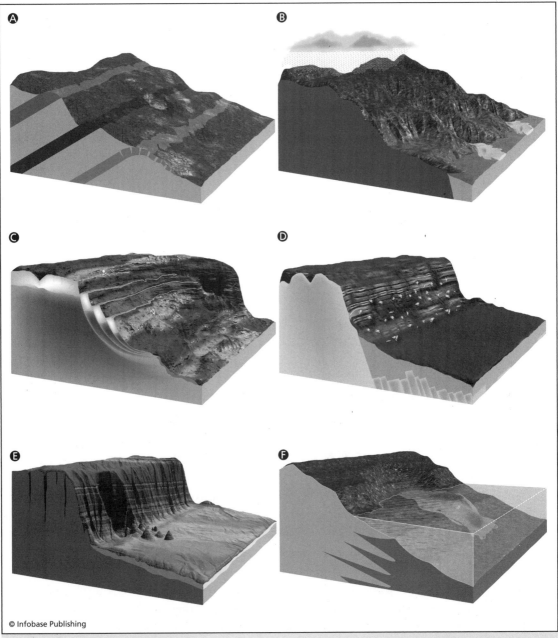

© Infobase Publishing

Types of mass wasting. Classification is based on the material that is moving, water content, and speed. A shows creep, the slow downslope movement of regolith; B shows a debris flow, the rapid downslope movement of rock and soil with water; C illustrates a slump, the downslope movement of coherent blocks of rocks or soil on curved fault surfaces; D illustrates a rockslide, the rapid downslope movement of rocks sliding along a rock surface such as a joint or bedding surface; E shows a rockfall, the free fall of rock or debris; and F is a subaqueous flow of sand or silt, typically becoming a turbidity current.

SLUMPS

A slump is a type of sliding slope failure in which a downward and outward rotational movement of rock or regolith occurs along a concave up slip surface. This produces either a singular or a series of rotated blocks, each with the original ground surface tilted in the same direction. Slumps are especially common after heavy rainfalls and earthquakes, and they can often be seen along roadsides and other slopes that have been artificially steepened to make room for buildings or other structures. Slump blocks may continue to move after the initial sliding event, and, in some cases, this added slippage is enhanced by rainwater that falls on the back-tilted surfaces and infiltrates along the fault, acting as a lubricant for added fault slippage.

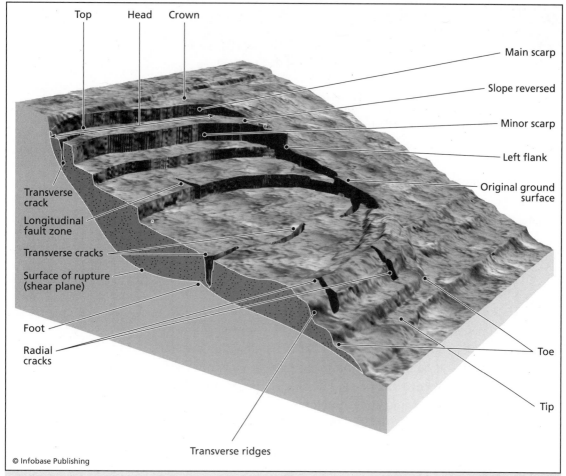

© Infobase Publishing

Geometry of a slump showing headwall scarp, listric normal fault, and toe

Slump showing a well-developed pressure ridge at the toe *(USGS)*

The 1964 magnitude 9.2 earthquake in Alaska triggered one of the more spectacular examples of slumping in modern times. The Turnagain Heights neighborhood that overlooked the scenic Cook Inlet, with the Alaska Range and Aleutian volcanoes in the background, was built on a series of layered rocks. One unit, known as the Bootlegger Shale, is weak and acts like quicksand when it is shaken (a process known as liquefaction). When the earthquake struck, the Bootlegger Shale was unable to support overlying rock layers and they all moved toward Cook Inlet on a series of tilted slump blocks. The entire neighborhood of Turnagain Heights sat on top of the slumped blocks, and houses were tilted on the surfaces of the slump blocks, twisted, and slid toward the inlet. Seventy homes in the Turnagain Heights neighborhood were destroyed, killing three people in the twisted buildings. The entire neighborhood was condemned, bulldozed, and is now a park called Earthquake Park.

A *translational slide* is a variation of a slump in which the sliding mass moves not on a curved surface, but downslope on a preexisting plane, such as a weak bedding plane or a joint. Translational slides may remain relatively coherent or break into small blocks forming a debris slide. The Vaiont Dam disaster of 1963 in Italy was one of the most deadly translational slides in recent history, killing more than 3,000 people. In this event, huge sections of the walls of a valley slid into a reservoir, creating a huge wave that destroyed several villages, resulting in many casualties. The slide occurred along curved bedding plane surfaces that dipped in toward the center of the valley, recently dammed to form a reservoir. The steep dip of rocks into the valley, plus lubrication and loading on the dipping planes by water, helped to initiate the slide, with disastrous results. This event is described in more detail in chapter 6.

SEDIMENT FLOWS

When mixtures of rock debris, water, and air begin to move under the force of gravity, they are said to flow. This is a type of deformation that is continuous and irreversible. The way in which this mixture flows depends on the relative amounts of solid, liquid, and air, the grain size distribution of the solid fraction, and the physical and chemical properties of the sediment. Mass wasting flows are transitional with stream-type flows, with changes in the amounts of sediment/water and in velocity. There are many names for the different types of *sediment flows,* including slurry flows, mudflows, debris flows, debris avalanches, *earthflows,* and loess flows. Many mass movements begin as one type of flow and evolve into another during the course of the mass wasting event. For instance, it is common for flows to begin as rockfalls or debris avalanches and evolve into debris avalanches, debris flows, and mudflows along their length as the flows pick up water and debris and flow over different slopes.

Earthflows are generally slow moving and form on moderate slopes with adequate moisture and fine-grained deformable soils such as clays and rocky soils with a silt or clay matrix. Earthflows can contribute large amounts of sediment to streams and rivers and typically move in short periods of episodic movement or relatively steady movement in response to heavy rainfall events, earthquakes, new irrigation works, or other disturbances. Most earthflows move along a basal shear surface and are characterized by internal deformation of the sliding material. Most earthflows do not fail catastrophically, but do cause significant damage to infrastructure.

CREEP

Creep is the imperceptible slow downslope flowing movement of regolith. It involves the very slow plastic deformation of the regolith, as well as repeated microfracturing of bedrock at nearly imperceptible rates. Creep occurs throughout the upper parts of the regolith where there is no single surface along which slip has occurred. Creep rates range from a fraction of an inch to about 2 inches per year on steep slopes. Creep accounts for leaning telephone poles, fences, and many of the cracks in sidewalks and roads. Although creep is slow and not very spectacular, it is one of the most important mechanisms of mass wasting and accounts for the greatest total volume of material moved downhill in any given year. One of the most common creep mechanisms is through frost heaving. Creep through frost heaving is extremely effective at moving rocks, soil, and regolith downhill because when the ground freezes, ice crystals form and grow, pushing rocks upward perpendicular to the surface. As the ice melts in the freeze-thaw cycle, gravity takes over and the pebble or rock moves vertically downward, ending up a fraction of an inch downhill from where it started. Creep can also be initiated by other mechanisms of surface expansion and contraction, such as warming and cooling, or the expansion and contraction of clay minerals with changes in moisture levels. In a related phenomenon, the freeze-thaw cycle can push rocks upward through the soil profile, as revealed in farmers' fields in New England and other northern climates where the fields seem to grow boulders. The fields are cleared of rocks, and, years later, the same fields are filled with more boulders. In these cases, the freezing forms ice crystals below the boulders

The effects of creep on railroad tracks in Canada, 1907 *(USGS)*

Solifluction lobes at Chicken Creek, Alaska, developed over permafrost *(USGS)*

that push them upward and, during the thaw cycle, the ice around the edges of the boulder melt first and mud and soil seep down into the crack and spaces along the edges of the boulders and find their way beneath the boulder. This process, repeated over years, is able to lift boulders to the surface, keeping the northern farmer busy.

The operation of the freeze-thaw cycle makes rates of creep faster on steep slopes than on gentle slopes, and faster with more water and greater numbers of freeze-thaw cycles. Rates of creep of up to half an inch per year are common.

SOLIFLUCTION

Solifluction is the slow viscous downslope movement of water-logged soil and debris. Solifluction is most common in polar latitudes where the top layer of permafrost melts, resulting in a water-saturated mixture resting on a frozen base. It is also common in very wet climates like the Tropics. Rates of movement are typically one to two inches (2.5–5 cm) per year, which is slightly faster than downslope flow by creep. Solifluction results in distinctive surface features such as lobes and sheets carrying the overlying vegetation. Sometimes, the lobes override each other, forming complex structures. Solifluction lobes are relatively common sights on mountainous slopes in wet climates, especially in areas with permafrost. The frozen layer beneath the soil prevents drainage of water deep into the soil or into the bedrock, so the uppermost layers in permafrost terrains tend to be saturated with water, aiding solifluction.

SLURRY FLOWS

A *slurry flow* is a moving mass of sediment saturated in water that is transported with the flowing mass. The mixture, however, is so dense that it can suspend large boulders or roll them along the base. When slurry flows stop moving, the resulting deposit therefore consists of a nonsorted mass of mud, boulders, and finer sediment.

DEBRIS FLOWS

Debris flows involve the downslope movement of unconsolidated regolith, most of which is coarser than sand. Some begin as slumps, but then continue to flow downhill as debris flows. They typically fan out and come to rest when they emerge out of steeply sloping mountain valleys onto flatter plains. Rates of movement in debris flows vary from several feet per year to several hundred miles per hour. Debris flows are commonly shaped like a tongue with numerous ridges and depressions. Many form after heavy rainfalls in mountainous areas, and the number of debris flows is increasing with greater deforestation of mountains and hilly areas. This is particularly obvious in Madagascar, where deforestation has taken place at an alarming rate, removing most of the island's trees. What was once a tropical rain forest is now a barren (but geologically spectacular) landscape, carved by numerous landslides and debris flows that bring the terra rosa soil to rivers, making them run red to the sea.

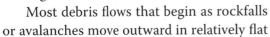

Debris flow, New Zealand *(Photo Researchers, Inc.)*

Most debris flows that begin as rockfalls or avalanches move outward in relatively flat terrain less than twice the distance they fell. Internal friction between particles in the flow and external friction especially along the base of the flow slow them. However, some of the largest debris flows that originated as avalanches or debris falls travel exceptionally large distances at high velocities—these are described in the following section called Debris Avalanches.

MUDFLOWS

Mudflows resemble debris flows, except that they have higher concentrations of water (up to 30 percent) that make them more fluid, with a consistency ranging from soup to wet concrete. Mudflows often start as a muddy stream in a dry mountain canyon, which picks up more and more mud and sand as it moves, until eventually the front of the stream is a wall of moving mud and rock. When this comes out of the canyon, the wall commonly breaks open, spilling the water behind it in a gushing flood, which moves the mud around on the valley floor. These types of deposits form many of the gentle slopes at the bases of mountains in the southwest United States.

Mudflows have become a hazard in highly urbanized areas such as Los Angeles, where most of the dry riverbeds have been paved over and development has moved into the mountains surrounding the basin. The rare rainfall events in these areas have no place to infiltrate and rush rapidly into the city, picking up all kinds of street mud and debris and forming walls of moving mud that cover streets and low-lying homes in debris. Unfortunately, after the storm rains and water recede, the mud remains and hardens in place. Mudflows are also common with the first heavy rains after prolonged droughts or fires, as residents of many California towns know. After the drought and fires of 1989 in Santa Barbara, heavy rains brought mudflows down out of the mountains filling the riverbeds and inundating homes with many feet of mud. Similar mudflows followed the heavy rains in Malibu in 1994, which remobilized barren soil exposed by the fires of 1993. Three to four feet of mud filled many homes and covered parts of the Pacific Coast Highway. Mudflows are part of the natural geologic cycle in mountainous areas, and they serve to maintain equilibrium between the rate of uplift of the mountains and their erosion. Mudflows are only catastrophic when people have built homes, highways, and businesses in places that mudflows must go.

Volcanoes, too, can produce mudflows. Layers of ash and volcanic debris, sometimes mixed with snow and ice, are easily remobilized by rain or by an eruption and may travel many miles. Volcanic mudflows are known as *lahars.* Mudflows have killed tens of thousands of people in single events and have been some of the most destructive of mass movements. Several instances are discussed in chapter 6.

GRANULAR FLOWS AND EARTHFLOWS

Granular flows are unlike slurry flows, since in granular flows the full weight of the flowing sediment is supported by grain-to-grain contact between individual grains. Earthflows are relatively fast granular flows with velocities ranging from three feet (1 m)/day to 1,200 feet (360 m) / hour.

ROCKFALLS AND DEBRIS FALLS

Rockfalls are the free fall of detached bodies of bedrock from a cliff or steep slope. They are common in areas of very steep slopes, where they may form huge deposits of boulders at the base of cliffs. Rockfalls can involve a single boulder or the entire face of a cliff. Debris falls are similar to rockfalls, but these consist of a mixture of rock and weathered debris and regolith.

Rockfalls have been responsible for the destruction of parts of many villages in the Alps, Andes, and other steep mountain ranges, and rockfall deposits have dammed many a river valley, creating lakes behind the newly fallen mass. Some of these natural dams have been extended and

THE WORLD BANK SUPPORTS DISASTER HAZARD MITIGATION PROJECT IN KYRGYZ REPUBLIC

In some places in the world, mass wasting is carrying more than natural regolith downhill. Buildings, neighborhoods, and historic landmarks have been lost to mass wasting. A potentially terrible situation is brewing in some of the former Soviet republics, where many years of disregard for the environment are starting to pose major threats to human health and safety. In Kyrgyzstan, landslides are threatening a nuclear waste disposal site on the side of a river where 2.6 million cubic yards (2 million cubic m) of waste were improperly disposed. A landslide on April 5, 2005, just missed sending the entire site into the river. New landslides appear imminent and could wash the waste into the river, which then drains into heavily populated Kergana Valley.

The World Bank has funded a $6.9 million grant to the Kyrgyz Republic in support of a Disaster Hazard Mitigation Project. The project aims at minimizing the exposure of humans and livestock to radionuclides associated with abandoned uranium mine tailings and waste rock dumps, improving the effectiveness of emergency management and response by national and subnational authorities and local communities to disaster situations, and reducing the loss of life and property in key landslide areas of the country.

The project comprises key mitigation measures designed to

- isolate and protect abandoned uranium mine tailings and waste dumps from disturbance by natural processes such as landslides, floods, and from leaching and dispersal processes associated with ground- and surface water drainage
- create an effectively administered disaster management and response system
- develop and implement systems to detect and warn against active landslide movements

"The project combines a mix of short- and long-term physical interventions as well as a number of institutional development activities," said Joop Stoutjesdijk, task team leader of the project. "The Ministry of Ecology and Emergency Situations is pleased that a large portion of the grant funds will be used for civil works aimed at isolation and protection of abandoned uranium mine tailings and waste rock dumps in the Mailuu-Suu area from landslides and floods," said Minister Temirbek Akmataliev. "It is indeed important that early measures are taken to improve the situation in Mailuu-Suu and ensure the population that the government is committed to improve the precarious situation with mine tailings," Stoutjesdijk noted. It is equally important that a start is made about warning populations against landslides that kill tens of rural people every year.

heightened by engineers to make reservoirs, including Lake Bonneville on the Columbia River and the Cheakamus Dam in British Columbia. Smaller examples abound in many mountainous terrains.

A spectacular rockfall in 1965 covered the Canadian town of Hope with 52,000,000 cubic yards (39,520,000 cubic m) of debris. This rockfall was caused by the construction of a highway through steep mountains made of rocks with a strong layering (schistosity) oriented roughly parallel to the slope of the mountains. After construction of the highway, minor ground shaking caused by snow avalanches apparently initiated the huge landslide that covered a two-mile-long section of the road with more than 250 feet (76 m) of debris, killing four people.

A large rockfall recently rocked Yosemite Valley, California, killing one visitor. At 6:52 P.M. on July 10, 1996, 162,000 tons of granite suddenly fell off Glacier Point, first sliding down a steep slope for more than 500 feet (152 m), then falling off an overhang and flying through the air at 270 MPH (435 km/hr) another 1,640 feet (500 m) before hitting the valley floor. Upon impact, the granite was pulverized and formed a huge dust cloud that rose more than half a mile high and shot across the valley knocking down 1,000 trees in its path and covering 50 acres of the scenic valley with an inch-thick layer of granitic dust.

Rock glacier on McCarthy Creek, central Alaska *(USGS)*

ROCKSLIDES AND DEBRIS SLIDES

Rockslides is the term given to the sudden downslope movement of newly detached masses of bedrock (or debris slides, if the rocks are mixed with other material or regolith). These are common in glaciated mountains with steep slopes and also in places where planes of weakness such as bedding planes, or fracture planes, dip in the direction of the slope. Like rockfalls, rockslides may form fields of huge boulders coming off mountain slopes. The movement to this talus slope is by falling, rolling, and sliding, and the steepest angle at which the debris remains stable is known as the angle of repose. The angle of repose is typically 33–37 degrees for most rocks.

Chaotic breccia, vent facies deposits consisting of volcanic bombs, cognate blocks, and lapilli mixed with accidental sedimentary blocks in a fine-grained tufaceous matrix, Glacier National Park, Montana *(USGS)*

A spectacular rockslide buried the coal-mining town of Frank, Alberta, Canada, on April 29, 1903. The town was built in the Oldham River Valley, along the base of a beautiful mountain known as Turtle Mountain. Turtle Mountain is made of steeply sloping limestone, underlain by weak shale, sandstone, and coal. At 4:10 A.M., 90 million tons of Turtle Mountain suddenly slid 3,000 feet (914 m) down into the valley, becoming instantly pulverized, and then moving two miles across the valley and coming to rest 400 feet (122 m) up the opposite mountain slope. The slide took about one-and-a-half minutes to fall from the mountain and move up the next slope. Seventy people lost their lives in the burial of Frank, and the town virtually vanished beneath the debris.

DEBRIS AVALANCHES

Debris avalanches are granular flows moving at very high velocity and covering large distances. These are rare but incredibly destructive and spectacular events. Some have ruined entire towns, killing tens of thousands of people without warning. Some have been known to move as fast as 250 miles per hour (403 km/hr). These avalanches can move so fast that they move down one slope, then thunder right up and over the next slope and into the next valley. One theory of why these avalanches move so fast is that when the rocks first fall, they trap a cushion of air and then travel on top of it like a hovercraft.

Two of the worst debris avalanches in recent history originated from the same mountain, Nevados Huascarán, the highest peak in the Peruvian Andes. Nevados Huascarán is made of granite and is cut by many vertical joint surfaces, forming many planes of weakness. At 6:13 P.M. on January 10, 1962, a huge mass of rock and ice fell off Nevados Huascarán. It formed a debris flow that moved into the valley below at 105 miles per hour (169 km/hr), coming to rest as a several square mile, 30–50-foot-thick (9–15 m) pile of rock and debris, covering parts of the town of Ranrahirca. Four thousand people died in this event, and survivors looked toward the scarred mountain with feelings of foreboding. They were right to be afraid.

On May 31, 1970, a large earthquake off the coast of Peru initiated another larger debris flow from Nevados Huscarán. The entire face of the mountain between elevations of 18,000 and 21,000 feet

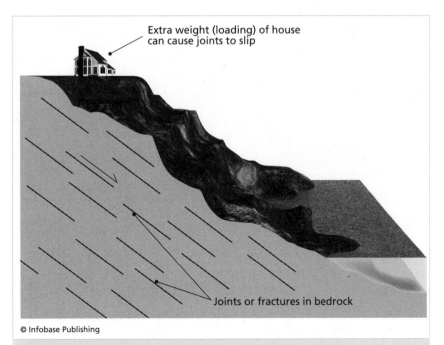

Extra weight (loading) of house can cause joints to slip

Joints or fractures in bedrock

© Infobase Publishing

Sketch of joints on a cliff in an orientation that promotes mass wasting. Extra loading by the weight of the house, particularly in times of heavy rainfall, may cause the joints to slip, generating a mass wasting event and sending the house into the ocean.

Debris avalanche in Leyte, Philippines, February 17, 2006, buried the town of Barangay Guinsaugon, killing 1,450 people. Would-be rescuers in this photo are moving boulders trying to uncover a school full of students and teachers. *(Associated Press)*

(5,486–6,400 m) collapsed, releasing more than 300 million cubic feet (9 million cubic m) of rock and ice that moved down the valley at 175–210 MPH (282–338 km/hr). This avalanche and debris flow covered a larger area, including many villages and the city of Yungay, killing more than 18,000 people in a few short minutes.

On February 17, 2006, another disastrous rockfall turned debris avalanche buried the town of Barangay Guinsaugon in Leyte, Philippines. This debris avalanche killed 1,450 people, amounting to most of the village, and led to frantic rescue efforts to save villagers and school-children who were trapped alive in a school beneath the debris. All efforts failed, despite the massive effort.

Conclusion

There is a wide range in the types of downslope movements known as mass wasting events. Some processes such as creep move at imperceptible rates of only one inch (2.5 cm) or so per year, whereas others such as debris avalanches can move at 200 MPH (322 km/hr) and cause catastrophic destruction to communities in the path of the flow. Some downslope flows involve only bedrock and are known as rockfalls if the rocks fall freely, or rockslides if they slide downhill along preexisting planes of weakness. Debris falls and debris slides involve rock and regolith. There is also a range in the amount of water present in downslope flows, from dry granular flows to wet mudslides and lahars that have large amounts of water mixed with mud and rock debris. Some downslope movements such as slumps do not travel far from the slope they were detached from, whereas others such as debris avalanches and mudflows may move many times the distance they fell, often many miles past their source onto adjacent lowlands.

5

Undersea Landslides

Mass wasting is not confined to the land. Submarine mass movements are common and widespread on the continental shelves, slopes, and rises, and also in lakes. Mass movements underwater, however, typically form *turbidity currents,* which leave large deposits of graded sand and shale. Under water, these slope failures can begin on very gentle slopes, even of less than one degree. Other submarine slope failures are similar to slope failures on land.

Slides and slumps and debris flows are also common in the submarine realm. Submarine deltas, deep-sea trenches, and continental slopes are common sites of submarine slumps, slides, and debris flows. Some of these are huge, covering hundreds of square miles. Many of the mass wasting events that produced these deposits must have produced large *tsunamis.* The continental slopes are cut by many canyons, produced by submarine mass wasting events, which carried material eroded from the continents into the deep ocean basins.

Triggering Mechanisms for Submarine Mass Wasting

Submarine mass wasting events are triggered by many phenomena, some similar to those on land. Shaking by earthquakes and displacement by faulting can initiate submarine mass wasting events, as can rapid release of water during sediment compaction. High sedimentation rates in deltas, continental shelves, and slopes, and other depositional environments may create unstable slopes that can fail spontaneously or through triggers including agitation by storm waves. In some instances, sudden release of methane and other gases in the submarine realm may trigger mass wasting events.

Submarine landslides tend to be larger than avalanches that originate above the waterline. Many submarine landslides are earthquake induced; others are triggered by storm events and by increases in pressure induced by sea-level rise on the sediments on *passive margins* or *continental shelves*. A deeper water column above the sediments on a shelf or slope environment can significantly increase the pressure in the pores of these sediments, causing them to become unstable and slide downslope. After the last glacial retreat 6,000–10,000 years ago, sea levels have risen by 320–425 feet (98–130 m), which has greatly increased the pore pressure on continental slope sediments around the world. This increase in pressure is thought to have initiated many submarine landslides, including the large Storegga slides more than 8,000 years ago off the coast of Norway.

Many areas beneath the sea are characterized by steep slopes, including areas along most continental margins, around islands, and along *convergent plate boundaries*. Sediments near deep-sea trenches are often saturated in water and close to the point of failure, where the slope gives out and collapses, causing the pile of sediments to suddenly slide down to deeper water depths. When an earthquake strikes these areas, large parts of the submarine slopes may give out simultaneously, often generating a tsunami.

Some steep submarine slopes that are not characterized by earthquakes may also be capable of generating huge tsunamis. Recent studies along the East Coast of North America, off Atlantic City, New Jersey, have revealed that large sections of the continental shelf and slope are on the verge of failure. The submarine geology off the coast of eastern North America consists of a several-thousand-feet-thick pile of unconsolidated sediments on the continental slope. These sediments are so porous and saturated with water that the entire slope is near the point of collapsing under its own weight. A storm or minor earthquake could be enough to trigger a giant submarine landslide in this area, possibly generating a tsunami that could sweep across the beaches of Long Island, New Jersey, Delaware, and much of the rest of the East Coast. With rising sea levels, the pressure on the continental shelves is increasing, and storms and other events may more easily trigger submarine landslides. This scary scenario is discussed in the following sidebar on sea level rise.

Storms are capable of generating submarine landslides even if the storm waves do not reach and disrupt the seafloor. Large storms are associated with storm surges that form a mound of water in front of the storm that may sometimes reach 20–32 feet (6–10 m) in height. As the storm surge moves onto the continental shelf, it is often preceded by a drop in sea level caused by a drop in air pressure, so the storm surge may be associated with large pressure changes on the seafloor and in the pores of unconsolidated sediments. A famous example of a storm surge–induced submarine landslide and tsunami is the catastrophic events in Tokyo, Japan, on September 1, 1923. On this day, a powerful typhoon swept across Tokyo, followed that evening by a huge submarine landslide and earthquake that generated a 36-foot- (11-m-) tall tsunami that swept across Tokyo, killing 143,000 people. Surveys of the seabed after the tsunami revealed that large sections slid out to

WILL SEA LEVEL RISE TRIGGER MORE SUBMARINE LANDSLIDES AND TSUNAMIS?

Rising sea levels may increase the number of catastrophic submarine landslides along the Atlantic and other seaboards, initiating tsunamis and causing widespread destruction. Submarine landslides can be generated by earthquakes, storm events, and increases in pressure on the sediments of the continental shelf from rises in sea level. Increases of water depths above the sediments on shelf or slope environments can significantly increase the pressure in the pores of these sediments, causing them to become unstable and slide downslope. After the last glacial retreat 6,000–10,000 years ago, sea levels have risen by 320–425 feet (98–130 m), which has greatly increased the pore pressure on continental slope sediments around the world. This increase in pressure is thought to have initiated many submarine landslides, including large submarine slides more than 8,000 years ago off the coast of Norway that generated tsunamis that swept the shores of the North Sea and Atlantic Ocean. Sea levels are presently rising about an inch every 10 years, but the rate is accelerating so that in the next hundred years sea levels will be three or four feet higher. This number could drastically change if, as some climate models predict, the Greenland or Antarctic ice caps suddenly and catastrophically melt. In those scenarios, sea levels will rise many tens, even hundreds, of feet over a lifetime. If that happens, cities including New Orleans, Miami, New York, Los Angeles, and Houston will be under water. Many sites around the margins of the ocean basins that are presently precariously near the verge of failure would see pore pressures increase, resulting in slope failures, massive submarine landslides, and more tsunamis sweeping the landward-moving shoreline.

Dramatic examples of submarine landslides caused by rising sea levels and increasing pressure on a continental shelf are provided by the Storegga slides of Norway. The eastern coast of Norway has been the site of several large submarine landslides that have sent tsunamis raging across the Norwegian and North Seas and into the open Atlantic. The largest of these are the Storegga slides, where masses of sediment slid from the shelf to deepwater at rates of 160 feet per second (50 m/sec), or 109 MPH (175 km/hr), depositing 250–1,500-foot- (80–450-m-) thick slide deposits at the base of sea, deepening the bay in many places by 300–650 feet (91–198 m), and locally by as much as 1,300 feet (396 m). Similar storm-induced slides are known from many continental slopes and delta environments, including the Mississippi Delta in the Gulf of Mexico and the coasts of Central America.

Types of Submarine Landslides

Submarine slides are part of a larger group of processes that can move material downslope on the seafloor and include other related processes such as slumps, debris flows, grain flows, and turbidity currents. Submarine slumps are a type of sliding slope failure in which a downward and outward rotational movement of the slope occurs along a concave up slip surface. This produces either a singular or a series of rotated

the slope and forming turbidite layers up to 65 feet (20 m) thick that traveled 300 miles (500 km) into the Norwegian Sea. The first well-documented slide occurred about 30,000 years ago, when about 930 cubic miles (3,880 cubic km) of sediment suddenly slipped down the steep continental slope. At this time, sea levels were low because much of the world's ocean water was being used to make the continental glaciers that covered much of North America, Europe, and Asia. Therefore, the tsunami resulting from this slide did not affect the present-day coastline. However, two more recent slides at Storegga, occurring between 8,000 and 6,000 years ago, struck during higher sea levels and left a strong imprint on the modern coastline. These slides probably were generated by the increase in pore pressure associated with rising sea levels, on a part of the continental shelf that was already on the verge of failure. The latter two slides were much smaller than the first, involving a total of 400 cubic miles (1,700 cubic km) of sediment. The second slide has been dated to have happened more than 8,000 years ago and had a height in the open ocean at its source of 25–40 feet (8–12 m). The waves crashed into Iceland, Greenland, and Scotland within a couple of hours. Greenland and Iceland saw the maximum run-up heights of 30–50 feet (10–15 m), and the waves refracted into the North Sea, causing variable run-ups of 10–65 feet (3–20 m) on the north coast of Scotland. The wide range in run-up heights is due to the variable topography of the coast of Scotland, and some uncertainty in the models of calculating run-up heights. These tsunamis scoured the coastline of Scotland and deposited tsunami sands and gravels 30–60 feet (10–20 m) above sea level in many places.

The Storegga slides provide historical evidence that areas along continental shelves that are close to the point of failure are particularly susceptible to collapse when sea levels rise and increase the pore pressure on the shelf. Increases in pore pressure reduce the strength of the sedimentary pile and make the shelf become metastable. At that point, relatively small disturbances, such as storms or minor earthquakes, could send huge sections of the shelf collapsing into deep water, generating tsunamis. Since many places along the eastern and western seaboards of North America and along the Gulf of Mexico are close to the point of failure, rising sea levels may equal an increase in the number of tsunamis affecting coastal regions.

blocks, each with the original seafloor surface tilted in the same direction. Slumps can move large amounts of material short distances in short times and are capable of generating tsunamis. Debris flows involve the downslope movement of unconsolidated sediment and water, most of which is coarser than sand. Some debris flows begin as slumps, but then continue to flow downslope as debris flows. They fan out and come to rest when they emerge out of submarine canyons onto flat *abyssal plains* on the deep seafloor. Rates of movement in debris flows vary from several feet per year to several hundred MPH. Debris flows are commonly shaped like a tongue with numerous ridges and depressions. Large debris flows can suddenly move large volumes of sediment, so are also capable of generating tsunamis. Turbidity currents are sudden movements of water-saturated sediments that move downhill under-

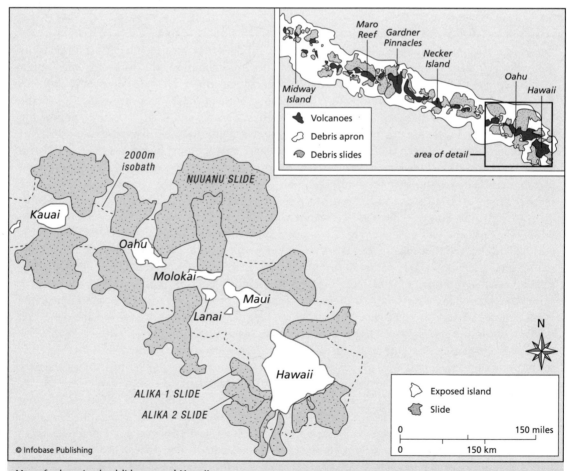

Map of submarine landslides around Hawaii

Image showing undersea topography off Los Angeles. Note the large submarine canyon with giant blocks transported by submarine landslides in the right-center of image; submarine slump and debris flows with headwall amphitheaters on the slope on the right-hand side of image; and oversteepened slope that could collapse any time along the left half of the image. *(USGS)*

water under the force of gravity. These form when water-saturated sediment on a shelf or shallow water setting is disturbed by a storm, earthquake, or some other mechanism that triggers the sliding of the sediment downslope. The sediment/water mixture then moves rapidly downslope as a density current and may travel tens or even hundreds of miles at tens of MPH until the slope decreases and the velocity of current decreases. As the velocity of the current decreases, the ability of the current to hold coarse material in suspension decreases. The current first drops its coarsest load, then progressively finer material as the current decreases further.

Many volcanic *hot spot* islands in the middle of some oceans show evidence that they repeatedly generate submarine landslides. These islands include Hawaii in the Pacific Ocean, the Cape Verde Islands in the North Atlantic, and Réunion in the Indian Ocean. These islands bear the telltale starfish shape with cuspate scars indicating the locations of old curved landslide surfaces. These islands are volcanically active, and *lava* flows move across their surfaces and then cool and crystallize quickly as the lava enters the water. This causes the islands to grow upward as very steep-sided columns, whose sides are prone to massive collapse and submarine sliding. Many volcanic islands are built up with a series of volcanic growth periods followed by massive submarine landslides, effectively widening the island as it grows. However, island growth by deposition of a series of volcanic flows over older landslide scars causes the island to be unstable—the old landslide scars are prone to later slip since they are weak surfaces and the added stress of the new material piled on top of them makes them more unstable. Other processes may also contribute to making these surfaces and the parts of the island above them unstable. For instance, on the Hawaiian Islands volcanic *dikes* have intruded along some old landslide scars, which can reduce the strength across the old surfaces by large amounts. Some parts of Hawaii are moving away from the main parts of the island by up to 0.5–4 inches per year (1–10 cm/yr) by the intrusion of volcanic dikes along old slip surfaces. Also, many landslide surfaces are characterized by accumulations of weathered material and blocks of rubble that under the additional weight of new volcanic flows can help to reduce the friction on the old slip surfaces, aiding the generation of new landslides. Therefore, as the islands grow, they are prone to additional large submarine slides that may generate tsunamis.

Conclusion

Continental shelves, slopes, rises, and outer trench slopes typically have very thick accumulations of sediments, many of which may be on the verge of slipping into deeper water. Submarine slumps, landslides, and debris flows can be activated by relatively minor shaking from earthquakes, volcanic eruptions, disturbances by deep storm waves, or by changes in the pressure on the loose sediments resting on the seafloor. The rise in sea level since the glaciers melted 10,000 years ago has raised sea levels, and the deeper water now exerts greater pressure on these thick piles of sediments. Therefore, many of these locations are unstable and can suffer mass wasting events with only minor disturbances.

Submarine mass wasting events tend to be larger than their land-based equivalents and may travel many tens of miles. The larger submarine landslides can generate tsunamis, so they pose significant risks to coastal communities. Even places such as the East Coast of the United States, where people feel relatively safe from tsunamis, are at risk for tsunamis generated by submarine landslides. Steep-sided volcanic islands in the middle of oceans pose significant risks as well, and landslides from these slopes could send tsunamis across ocean basins to shorelines hundreds or thousands of miles away.

6

Landslide Disasters

Mass wasting is one of the most costly natural hazards, with the slow downslope creep of material causing billions of dollars of damage to properties every year in the United States alone. Earth movements do not kill many people in most years, but occasionally massive landslides take thousands or even hundreds of thousands of lives. Mass wasting is becoming more of a hazard in the United States as people move in great numbers from the plains into mountainous areas as population increases. This trend is expected to continue in the future, and more mass wasting events like those described in this chapter may be expected every year. Good engineering practices and understanding of the driving forces of mass wasting will hopefully prevent many mass wasting events, but it will be virtually impossible to stop the costly gradual downslope creep of material, especially in areas with freeze-thaw cycles.

This chapter examines the details of a few of the more significant mass wasting events of different types, including a translational slide, a rockfall-debris avalanche, a mudflow, and a wholesale collapse of an entire region. Lessons that can be learned from each of these events are discussed with the aim that education can save lives in the future. The following table lists some of the more significant landslide and mass wasting disasters with more than 1,000 deaths reported, with a bias toward events of the last 100 years.

Some Significant Downslope Flows—in Terms of Deaths and Destruction

WHERE	WHEN	TRIGGER PROCESS	HOW MANY DEATHS
Shaanxi Province, China	1556	m. 8 earthquake	830,000
Shaanxi Province, China	1920	m. 8.6 earthquake	200,000
Nevados Huascarán, Peru	1970	m. 7.7 earthquake	70,000
Nevado del Ruiz, Colombia	1985	volcanic eruption	20,000
Tadzhik Republic	1949	m. 7.5 earthquake	12,000–20,000
Honduras, Nicaragua	1998	heavy rain	10,000
Venezuela	1999	*	10,000
Nevados Huascarán, Peru	1962	*	4,000–5,000
Vaiont, Italy	1963	heavy rain	3,000
Rio de Janeiro, Brazil	1966–7	heavy rain	2,700
Mount Coto, Switzerland	1618	*	2,430
Cauca, Colombia	1994	m. 6.4 earthquake	1,971
Serra das Araras, Brazil	1967	heavy rain	1,700
Leyte, Philippines	2006	heavy rain	1,450
Kure, Japan	1945	*	1,145
Shizuoka, Japan	1958	heavy rain	1,094
Rio de Janeiro, Brazil	1966	heavy rain	1,000
Napo, Ecuador	1987	m. 6.1 and 6.9 earthquakes	1,000

* cause unknown

Shaanxi, China, January 23, 1556

The deadliest earthquake and mass wasting event on record occurred on January 23, 1556, in the central Chinese province of Shaanxi. Most of the 830,000 deaths from this earthquake resulted from landslides and the collapse of homes built into *loess,* a deposit of windblown dust that covers much of central China. This loess is fine-grained soil eroded from the Gobi Desert to the north and west and deposited by wind on the great loess plateau of central China. Thus, although this disaster was triggered by an earthquake, mass wasting processes were actually responsible for most of the casualties.

The earthquake that triggered this disaster occurred on the morning of January 23, 1556, and it leveled a 520-mile- (837-km-) wide area and caused significant damage across 97 counties in the provinces of Shaanxi, Shanxi, Henan, Hebei, Hubei, Shandong, Gansu, Jiangsu, and

Map of China, showing the areas affected by the Shaanxi earthquakes of 1556 and 1920

House destroyed by landslide in Shaanxi Province, China, 2006 *(Landov)*

Anhui. Sixty percent of the population was killed in some counties. There were no seismic instruments at the time, but seismologists estimate that the earthquake had a magnitude of 8 on the Richter scale, with an epicenter near Mount Hua in Hua county in Shaanxi.

The reason for the unusually high death toll in this earthquake is because most people in the region at the time lived in homes carved out of the soft loess, or silty soil. People in the region would carve homes, called *yaodongs,* out of the soft loess and benefit from the cool summer temperatures and moderate winter temperatures of the soil. These caves would provide an escape from the sun and the blowing dust that characterizes the loess plateau. The shaking from the magnitude 8 earthquake caused huge numbers of these *yaodongs* to collapse, trapping the residents inside. Landslides raced down steep loess-covered slopes, and, because the shaking went on so long, even *yaodongs* in flat areas collapsed.

(opposite page) Map and cross section of Vaiont Dam disaster showing locations of the slide masses, reservoir, and towns devastated by the rockslide: (a) shows the distribution of the landslide mass that slid into reservoir, and the locations of Vaiont, Casso, Erto, and S. Martino that were destroyed or heavily damaged in the landslide and subsequent waves. (b) shows a cross section across the landslide mass and reservoir, illustrating the volume of material that slid, and the shape of the surface that the landslide mass moved along.

Time tends to make people forget about risks associated with natural hazards. For events that only occur every couple of hundred years, several generations may pass between catastrophic events and each generation remembers less about the risks than the previous one. This facet of human nature was unfortunately illustrated by another earthquake in central China nearly 400 years later. In 1920, a large earthquake in Haiyuan, in the Ningxia region of northern Shaanxi Province,

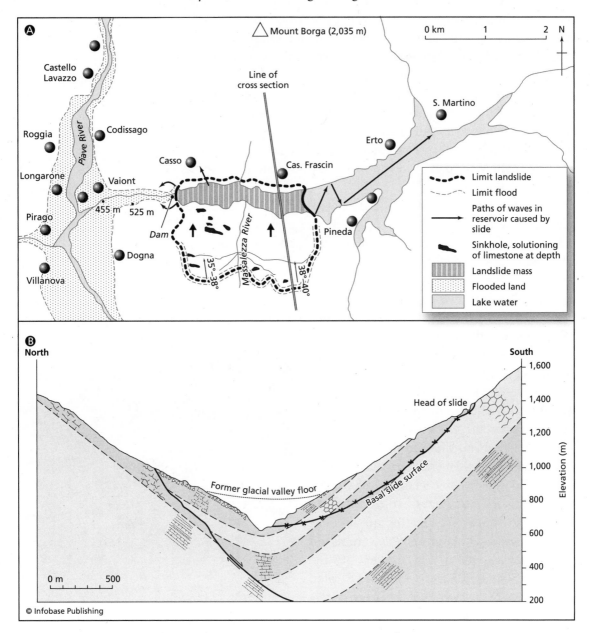

© Infobase Publishing

caused about 675 major landslides in deposits of loess, killing another 100,000–200,000 people.

Vaiont, Italy, October 9, 1963

One of the worst translational slides in history occurred in Vaiont, Italy, in 1963. In 1960, a large dam was built in a deep valley in northern Italy. The valley occupies the core of a synclinal fold in which the limestone rock layers dip inward toward the valley center and form steeply dipping bedding surfaces along the valley walls. The valley floor was filled with glacial sediments left as the glaciers from the last ice age departed a few thousand years ago. The bottom of the valley was oversteepened by downcutting from streams, forming a steep V-shaped valley in the middle of a larger U-shaped glacial valley. The rocks on the sides of the valley are highly fractured and broken into many individual blocks, and there was an extensive cave network carved in the limestone. The reservoir behind the dam held approximately 500 million cubic feet (14 million cubic m) of water.

After the dam was constructed, the pores and caves in the limestone filled with water, exerting extra, unanticipated pressures on the valley walls and dam. Heavy rains in the fall of 1963 made the problem worse, and authorities predicted that sections of the valley might experience landslides. The rocks on the slopes surrounding the reservoir began creeping downhill, first at a quarter-inch per day (.3–.65 cm/day), then accelerating to one-and-a-half inches per day (4 cm/day) by October 6. Even though authorities were expecting landslides, they had no idea of the scale of what was about to unfold.

At 10:41 P.M. on October 9, 1963, a 1.1-mile- (1.8-km-) long and 1-mile- (1.6-km-) wide section of the south wall of the reservoir suddenly failed and slid into the reservoir at more than 60 MPH (96 km/hr). Approximately 750 million cubic feet (2,250,000 cubic m) of debris fell into the reservoir, creating an earthquake shock and creating an air blast that shattered windows and blew roofs off nearby houses. The debris that fell into the reservoir displaced a huge amount of water, and a series of monstrous waves were generated that raced out of the reservoir, devastat-

Vaiont Dam rock slide and the debris that wrecked the towns around the reservoir in 1963 *(Corbis)*

ing nearby towns. A 780-foot- (238-m-) tall wave moved out of the north side of the reservoir, followed by a 328-foot- (100-m-) tall second wave. The waves combined and formed a 230-foot- (70-m-) tall wall of water that moved down the Vaiont Valley, inundating the town of Longarone, where more than 2,000 people were killed by the fast-moving floodwaters. Other waves bounced off the walls of the reservoir and emerged out the upper end of the reservoir, smashing into the town of San Martino where another 1,000 people were killed in the raging waters.

Landslides in the Andes Mountains; Nevados Huascarán, Peru, 1962, 1970

The steep Andes Mountains are in South America and are affected by frequent earthquakes and volcanic eruptions. They are glaciated in places and experience frequent storms because of their proximity to the Pacific Ocean. All of these factors result in many landslides and related mass wasting disasters in the Andes. Some of the most catastrophic landslides have emanated from Nevados Huascarán, a tall peak on the slopes of the Cordillera Blanca in the Peruvian province of Ancash. In 1962, a large debris avalanche with an estimated volume of 16,900,000 cubic yards (13,000,000 cubic m) rushed down the slopes of Nevados Huascarán at an average velocity of 105 MPH (170 km/hr). The debris avalanche buried the village of Ranrahirca, killing 4,000–5,000 people. This scene of devastation was to be repeated eight years later. On May 31, 1970, a magnitude 7.9 earthquake centered about 22 miles (35 km) offshore of Chimbote, a major Peruvian fishing port, caused widespread destruction and about 3,000 deaths in Chimbote. The worst destruction, however, was caused by a massive debris avalanche that rushed off Nevados Huascarán at 174 MPH (280 km/hr). This debris flow had a volume of 39,000,000–65,000,000 cubic yards (30–50,000,000 cubic m) and rushed through the Callejón de Huaylas, a steep valley that runs parallel to the coast. The debris avalanche covered the town of Yungay under thick masses of boulders, dirt, and regolith. Seventy percent of the buildings in the town were covered with tens of feet of debris. The death toll was enormous—most estimates place the deaths at 18,000, although local officials say that 20,000 died in Yungay alone, and as many as 70,000 people died in the region from the landslides associated with the May 31, 1970, earthquake.

There have been many other landslide disasters in the Andes Mountains. In 1974, a rock slide/debris avalanche in the Peruvian province of Huancavelica buried the village of Mayunmarca, killing 450 people. The

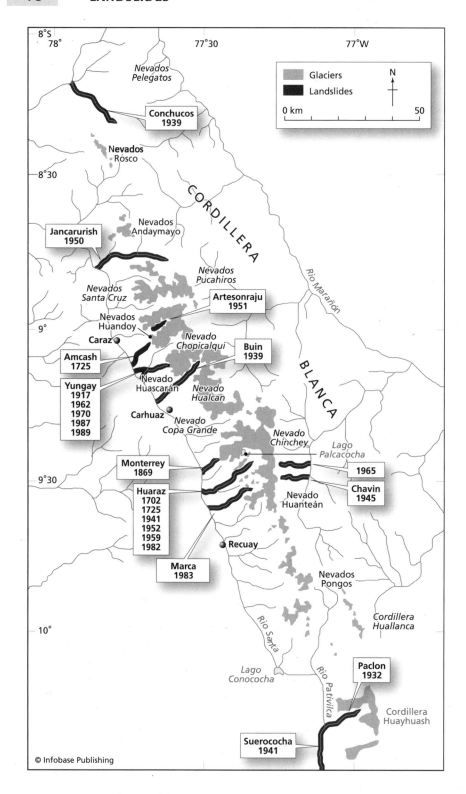

8°S
78°   77°30   77°W

Nevados Pelegatos

Conchucos 1939

Nevados Rosco

8°30

CORDILLERA

Nevados Andaymayo

Jancarurish 1950

Nevados Pucahiros

Nevados Santa Cruz

Artesonraju 1951

Nevados Huandoy

Caraz

Nevado Chopicalqui

Buin 1939

Amcash 1725

Nevado Huascarán

Nevado Hualcan

Yungay 1917 1962 1970 1987 1989

Carhuaz

Nevado Copa Grande

9°

Nevado Chinchey

Lago Palcacocha

Monterrey 1869

1965

Huaraz 1702 1725 1941 1952 1959 1982

Chavin 1945

Nevado Huanteán

Recuay

9°30

Marca 1983

Nevados Pongos

Cordillera Huallanca

BLANCA

Río Marañón

10°

Río Santa

Lago Conococha

Río Pativilca

Paclon 1932

Cordillera Huayhuash

Suerococha 1941

Glaciers
Landslides
0 km   50
N

© Infobase Publishing

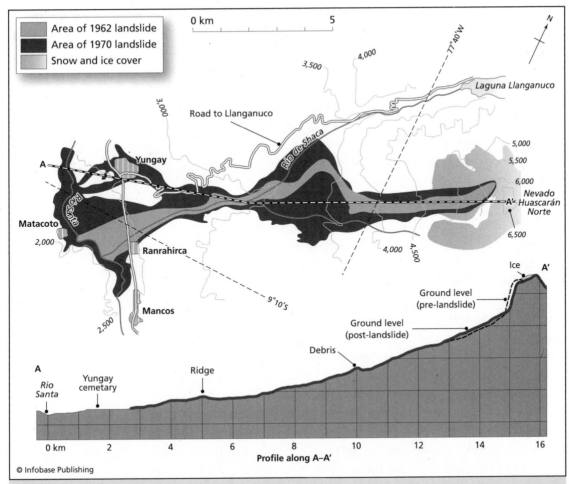

Detailed map and topographic profile of Nevados Huascarán, showing the deposits from the 1962 and 1970 landslides *(modeled after USGS)*

debris avalanche raced down the mountain with an average velocity of 87 MPH (140 km/hr) and caused the failure of a 492-foot- (150-meter-) high older landslide dam, initiating major downstream flooding. Debris with a volume of 16,000,000,000 cubic meters from the 1974 avalanche blocked the Mantaro River, creating a new lake behind the deposit. In 1987, the Reventador landslides in Napo, Ecuador, were triggered by two earthquakes with magnitudes of 6.1 and 6.9. These earthquakes mobi-

(opposite page) Map of the Cordillera Blanca, Río Santa valley of Peru, showing the glacier-covered peaks and numerous landslide deposits that have caused many disasters and killed tens of thousands of people. Nevados Huascarán is located in the center of the valley and has had major landslides in 1917, 1962, 1970, 1987, and 1999. *(modeled after USGS)*

lized 98,000,000–143,000,000 cubic yards (75–110,000,000 cubic m) of soil that was saturated with water on steep slopes. These slides remobilized into major debris flows along tributary and main drainages, killing 1,000 people and destroying many miles of the TransEcuador oil pipeline, the main economic lifeline for the country. The magnitude 6.4 Paez earthquake in Cauca, Colombia, in 1994 also initiated thousands of thin soil slides that grouped together and were remobilized into catastrophic debris flows in the larger drainages. As these raced downstream, 1,971 people were killed and more than 12,000 people were displaced from their destroyed homes.

Nevado del Ruiz, Colombia, November 10, 1985

The most deadly volcanic-induced mudflow disaster of modern times was started by a relatively minor eruption in the Andes of South America. The Nevado del Ruiz volcano in Colombia entered an active phase in November 1984 and began to show harmonic tremors on November 10, 1985. At 9:37 P.M., a large eruption sent an ash cloud several miles into the atmosphere, and this ash settled onto the ice cap on top of the mountain. The ash and volcanic steam quickly melted large amounts of the ice, which mixed with the ash and formed giant lahars (mudflows) that swept down the east side of the mountain into the village of Chinchiná, killing 1,800 people. The eruption continued and melted more ice that mixed with more ash and sent additional larger lahars westward. Some of these lahars moved nearly 30 miles (50 km) at nearly 30 MPH (50 km/hr). Under a thunderous roar, they buried the town of Armero under 26 feet (8 m) of mud, killing another 22,000 people. Many people could have been saved since warnings were issued before the mudflow, but they went unheeded.

Nevado del Ruiz had gone through a year of intermittent precursory activity that indicated that an eruption might occur, and the volcano was being studied by a group of Colombian geologists at the time of the eruption. At 3:05 P.M. on November 13, 1985, ranchers north of the volcano heard a low, rumbling noise and observed a plume of black ash rise from the volcano and fall on the town of Armero 45 miles (72 km) away about two hours later. By 4 P.M., local civil defense officials warned that an eruption was in progress and were recommending that towns including Armero, Honda, and others be ready for immediate evacuation. After several hours of meetings, the Red Cross ordered the evacuation of Armero at 7:30 P.M. However, residents did not hear the orders and did not understand the danger moving their way.

Nevados Huascarán, Peru, June 13, 1970. The 1970 debris avalanche destroyed the town of Yungay and much of the town of Ranrahirca (lower foreground), killing at least 18,000 people in these towns and up to 70,000 people in the whole valley. *(USGS, courtesy of Servicio Aerofotografico Nacional de Peru)*

At 9:08 P.M., two large explosions marked the start of a larger eruption, associated with a series of *pyroclastic* flows and surges that moved down the north flank of the volcano. The volcanic deposits moved across the ice cap on the mountain, scouring, melting, and covering it in various places. This released large amounts of meltwater mixed with debris that moved down the slopes, quickly forming giant lahars that scoured the channels of the Nereidas, Molinos, Guali, Azufrado, and Lagunillas Rivers, picking up huge amounts of debris including rocks, soil, and vegetation in the process. This mudflow picked up speed and raced downhill toward the villages built along the rivers.

A *Plinian* eruption column was visible by 9:30 P.M., rising to nearly 7 miles (11 km), and it was hurling blocks and bombs of andesitic pumice up to a couple of miles from the crater, with ash falling up to 250 miles (400 km) away. At 10:30 P.M., lahars began sweeping through the village of Chinchina, and additional warnings were sent to Armero. Later, survivors reported that electricity was out sporadically and many residents may not have heard the warnings. At 11:30, giant lahars surged into Armero in successive waves moving at 22–30 MPH (35–50 km/hr), sweeping away homes, cars, people, and livestock and embedding all in 26 feet (8 m) of mud. Many people survived the initial inundation but were trapped half-buried in the mud and died later of exposure.

Scientists have learned many lessons from Nevado del Ruiz that could be useful to save lives in the future. First, even minor volcanic eruptions can trigger catastrophic mudflows under the right conditions, and geologic hazard maps should be made in areas of volcanism to understand the hazards and help emergency planning in times of eruption. Local topographic variations can focus lahars, enhancing their lethality in some places and spreading them out in others. Armero was located at the end of a canyon that focused the worst parts of the flow in the heart of the village. Understanding past hazards can help understand what may happen in the future. If geologists had helped plan the location of Armero, they would have noticed that the town was placed on top of an older lahar deposit that swept down the mountain in 1845, also killing all inhabitants more than a century earlier. Apparently, the geologic record shows a number of repeated mudflows destroying villages at the site of Armero. A final lesson from Armero is that warning systems need to be in place, and even simple alarm systems can save thousands of lives. If residents of Armero had had even a one-hour warning they could have fled to the valley slopes and survived. The mudflows traveled 45 miles (70 km), taking about one-and-a-half hours to get to Armero, so even simple warnings could have saved lives.

Central America—Honduras, El Salvador, Nicaragua, October 1998

Hurricane Mitch devastated the Caribbean and Central American regions from October 24–31, 1998, striking as one of the strongest and most damaging storms to hit the region in more than 200 years. The storm reached hurricane status on October 24 and peaked on October 26–27 with sustained winds of 180 MPH (288 km/hr). The storm remained stationary off the coast of Honduras for more than 24 hours, then slowly moved inland across Honduras and Nicaragua, picking up additional moisture from the Pacific Ocean. The very slow forward movement of the storm produced unusually heavy precipitation even for a storm this size. Total amounts of rainfall have been estimated to range between 31–74 inches (80–190 cm) in different parts of the region. Most of the devastation from Mitch resulted from the torrential

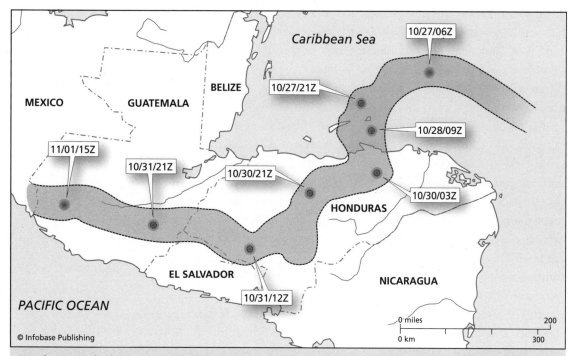

Map showing path of Hurricane Mitch through western Caribbean and Central America in October and November of 1998 (modeled after USGS)

rains associated with the storm, which continued to fall at a rate of 4 inches (10 cm) per hour even long after the storm moved overland and its winds diminished. The rains from Mitch caused widespread catastrophic floods and landslides throughout the region, affecting Honduras, Guatemala, Nicaragua, and El Salvador. These landslides buried people, destroyed property, and clogged drainages with tons of fresh sediment deposited in the rivers. More than 10,000 people were killed by flooding, landslides, and debris flows across the region, with 6,600 of the deaths reported from along the northern seaboard of Honduras. More than 3 million people were displaced from their homes. The crater of Casita volcano in Nicaragua filled up with water from the storm and ruptured, initiating large debris flows in this region.

The effects of Hurricane Mitch in Central America were unprecedented in the scope of damage from downed trees, floods, and landslides. Honduras suffered some of the heaviest rainfall, with three-day storm totals in the southern part of the country exceeding 36 inches (90 cm). The areas of heaviest rainfall experienced the greatest number of landslides. Most of the landslides were shallow debris flows with average thickness of only 3.3–6.6 feet (1–2 m), with runout distances of up to 1,000 feet (300 m). Landslide density in the southern part of Honduras reached about 750–800 square miles (300 sq km). In the capital of Tegucigalpa, most damage was caused by two large slump/earthflows and debris slides, with the largest being the Cerro El Berrinche slump/earthflow that destroyed Colonia Soto and parts of Colonias Catorce de Febrero and El Porvenir. This landslide moved about 7,800,000 cubic yards (6 million cubic m) of material downhill, damming the Rio Choluteca and creating a reservoir of stagnant, polluted, sewage-filled water behind the newly created dam. This landslide initially moved slowly, so residents were able to be evacuated prior to the time it accelerated and dammed the river. The landslide consisted of three main parts, including a toe of buckled and folded rock and regolith, then upslope a tongue of a mass of regolith that slid across and dammed the Rio Choluteca, and an upper part consisting of a giant slump block. Other rock and debris slides were triggered by erosion of riverbanks by floods, destroying more homes.

In El Salvador, flooding from the rain from Mitch did more damage than landslides, with landslides being more important in the north near the border with Honduras. Most of the storm-induced landslides in El Salvador were shallow features that displaced unconsolidated surface regolith derived from deep tropical weathering. Most of the landslides did not travel far but moved downhill as coherent masses that stopped at the bases of steep hills, becoming highly fragmented by the time they stopped moving. Some landslides were fluid enough to evolve into debris flows that traveled up to several miles from their sources, moving quickly across low-gradient slopes and into drainage

Landslide in El Salvador, January 2001. This earthquake-induced slide demolished much of the Las Colinas neighborhood of Santa Tecla, a suburb of San Salvador, the capital of El Salvador. *(Associated Press)*

networks. The largest landslide in El Salvador resulting from Mitch was the El Zompopera slide, a translational earth slide that evolved into a debris flow, traveling more than 3.7 miles (6 km) from its source. This slide was a preexisting feature whose growth was accelerated by Mitch. Other preexisting landslides also were remobilized as earth slides and earthflows, with rounded head scarps and hummocky topography. Landslides in El Salvador did much less damage than landslides in Honduras.

In Nicaragua, most of the landslides triggered by the rains from Hurricane Mitch were debris flows. These debris flows ranged from small flows that displaced only a few cubic meters of material to a depth of a few meters that moved a few tens of meters downslope, to larger debris flows covering 96,000 square yards (80,000 sq m) that moved material up to two miles (3 km) downslope in channels. The depth of landslide scars shows a clear relationship to the depth of weathered and altered material, with deeper weathering leading to deeper depths of landslides. In some areas, landslides covered 80 percent of the terrain, but the disturbed areas were considerably smaller in most locations. Hurricane Mitch also initiated some slow-moving earthflows that continued to move more than a year after the storm. Mapping of the substrate in Nicaragua has shown that soils and rocks of certain types were more susceptible to landslides than other materials, so risk maps for future rain-induced landslide events can be made.

One of the worst individual mass movement events associated with the torrential rains from Hurricane Mitch was the collapse of the water-filled *caldera* of Casita volcano. Water rushed out of the volcanic caldera as it collapsed, mixing with ash, soil, and debris that washed down rivers, destroying much in its path. Approximately 1,560–1,680 people were killed in this disaster, and many more were displaced. Several towns and settlements were completely destroyed and many bridges along the Pan-American Highway were destroyed. This was the worst disaster to affect Nicaragua since the 1972 Managua earthquake.

The Casita volcano is a convergent margin volcano, part of the Cordillera Maribos volcanic chain that extends from the northern shore of Lake Managua to Chinandega in the south. Casita is one of five main volcanic edifices and is a deeply dissected composite volcano that has a .6-mile- (1-km-) diameter crater at its summit. Heavy rainfall from Hurricane Mitch dropped 4 inches (10 cm) of rain per day on the summit starting on October 25, increasing to 8 inches (20 cm) per day by October 27, and reached a remarkable 20 inches (50 cm) per day on

October 30, 1998, the day of the avalanche. The normal monthly average rainfall for October is 13 inches (33 cm), so the rainfall on Casita was more than six times the normal level preceding the avalanche.

The avalanche began along an altered segment of rock along a fault that cuts the volcano about 66–88 yards (60–80 m) beneath the summit. The avalanche and release of water began when a slab of rock, measuring 137 yards (150 m) long, 55 yards (60 m) high, and 18 yards (20 m) thick, broke off this fault zone and slid down the fault surface at a 45-degree angle toward the southeast. This initial rockslide released about 260,000 cubic yards (200,000 cubic m) of rock.

Residents who lived below the volcano and survived reported a sound like a helicopter, along with minor round shaking, as the first avalanche was shattered into small pieces as the rock mass slid down the fault plane. For the first 1.3 miles (2 km), the avalanche deposit moved through a narrow valley, forming a mass of moving rock 500–825 feet (150–250 m) wide and 100–200 feet (30–60 m) deep. As the flow moved down the valley, it sloshed back and forth from side to side of the valley, bouncing off the steep walls as it roared past at 50 feet (15 m) per second, sending large blocks of rock flying 6–10 feet (2–3 m) into the air, decapitating trees above the valley floor. As it continued to move downhill, the blocks of rock in the avalanche scoured the clay-rich soil from the valley floor, excavating up to 33 feet (10 m) of material and incorporating this into the avalanche deposit. This process increased the volume of the downslope flow by about nine times its initial volume.

About three hours after the initial avalanche, a lahar was generated from the main accumulation of the avalanche rock, about two miles (3 km) from the summit and two miles above the towns of El Porvenir and Rolando Rodriquez. It is likely that the rain and river flow continued to build up in the avalanche deposit until the pressure inside was great enough to break through the debris-blocked front of the deposit. The lahar formed a rapidly moving concentrated flow that was about 10 feet (3 m) thick and spread across a width of almost a mile. As the lahar raced through the towns of El Porvenir and Rolando Rodriguez, it destroyed all buildings and signs of human habitation, scouring the soil and moving this with the flow. Approximately 2,000 people are thought to have perished in the lahar that wiped the two towns away, but the death toll is inaccurate, since the bodies were removed and burned for sanitary reasons before accurate counts were made. Several other smaller towns were also destroyed and a large agricultural area, including many livestock, was wiped out.

Warnings could have helped avoid the Casita disaster and the destruction of El Porvenir and Rolando Rodriguez. First, the towns were built in a low-lying area on deposits of old lahars, and the geologic risks should have been appreciated before the towns were settled. The incredibly high rainfall totals should have warned residents that the risks for landslides and lahars was high. Certainly after the avalanche occurred, stopping only two miles upstream, the residents should have been evacuated before the lahar surged out of the avalanche deposit. These risks should be assessed and applied to the other volcanoes in Central America, as similar situations exist in many places in this region. The horror of the Casita disaster can be appreciated in the dispatch to the Volcano Network in Managua, which is contained in the sidebar on page 89.

Leyte, Philippines, February 17, 2006

A massive landslide buried the community of Barangay Guinsaugon in the central Philippines on February 17, 2006, killing an estimated 1,450 people. This landslide is classified as a rock slide/debris avalanche, having started as a rock slide and turning into a debris avalanche as it moved downslope and spread across the adjacent lowland. The debris avalanche apparently rode on a cushion of air trapped beneath the falling regolith, enabling the avalanche to reach speeds of 87 MPH (140 km/hr) and completely destroying the village within 3–4 minutes from the time of the start of the rock slide.

The Philippines are cut by a major fault that strikes through the entire length of the island chain. This fault is active and related to the convergence and left-lateral strike slip motion between the Philippine plate and the Pacific plate, which is being subducted beneath the islands from the east. The Philippines are tectonically active, have many steep slopes, and experience heavy seasonal rainfall. All these factors can contribute to making slopes unstable and undoubtedly helped initiate the 2006 landslide. In the region of the massive rock slide/debris avalanche, the Philippine fault strikes north-northwest and a second fault branches off this toward the southeast. Movement along these faults has uplifted steep mountains, and these slopes show many horseshoe-shaped scars that probably represent a series of landslide scars.

The landslide covered an area of about 3,600,000 square yards (3,000,000 sq m) and stretches 2.5 miles (4 km) from the head of the scarp to the toe of the slide. Considering that the thickness of the deposit ranges from about 100 feet (30 m) at the base of the slope of

MUD AVALANCHE FROM CASITA VOLCANO, NICARAGUA

Report to Volcano Network, Managua, Sunday, November 1, 1998
From: Wilfried Strauch
Geophysical Department
Instituto Nicaraguense de Estudios Territoriales
Managua, Nicaragua

Heavy rainfalls related to Hurricane Mitch and lasting more than one week have caused inundations of large parts of central and northwestern Nicaragua. Rivers destroyed several important bridges; the Pan-American Highway between Honduras/El Salvador and Nicaragua is interrupted at many places. About 200 people were reported killed in the floods, in their collapsed houses or in minor mudflows. Traffic between Managua and the northern and northwestern departments, as Matagalpa, Esteli, Jinotega, Leon, Chinandega, is interrupted. Many of the isolated places suffer shortages of food. At several places people had to seek salvation on their roofs or on trees as the water level increased very fast. Tens of thousands lost their homes. Dramatic rescue operations took place, as for instance in Malacatoya, where a group of people was saved by a ship coming from Granada City. Malacatoya River had raised its level by more than 50 feet (15 m), the highways were overflooded and destroyed. At some places the landscape changed completely—rivers broadened their beds or united themselves with other rivers, as occurred in the area of Sebaco. New lakes were formed and mountains were washed away, collapsed and disappeared. Crops were largely destroyed. Helicopter-based rescue operations of the Nicaraguan Army were possible since yesterday when the meteorological conditions improved. Only today the dimension of a mud avalanche became clear which occurred already on Friday afternoon at Casita volcano. The mud covered an area of about 20 km length and 2–3 km width, southwest of the volcano. Numerous villages, settlements, and houses between Casita volcano and the town of Posoltega were destroyed.

Exact information about population density in this area does not exist but it is assumed that more than 1,000 people, maybe even 2,000, could have died. Today, Nicaraguan Army and Red Cross reported having found 400 cadavers. Rescue is very difficult because of the mud, and the rain continues. The Nicaraguan government declared Natural Disaster Emergency for the most affected regions of the country. The main tasks for the next days are the rescue of people who are still in danger, helicopter transports of food to the isolated places, and the preliminary repair of the communication lines. Due to this extreme disaster the Nicaraguan economy has certainly suffered a sensitive drawback. Thus, the repair of highways is now of extraordinary importance as the coffee harvest should begin in a few days.

the mountain to 20–23 feet (6–7 m) near the toe of the slide, it is estimated that about 19.5–26 million cubic yards (15–20 million cubic m) of material collapsed from the mountain on February 17, 2006. The velocity of the flow during the slide has been estimated at 60–87 MPH (100–140 km/hr), based on the time survivors remembered the event to take place in and the distance the material traveled.

The rock slide originated on the fault surface of the Philippine fault zone and excavated a large, horseshoe-shaped amphitheater on the side of the mountain at a height of about 2,228 feet (675 m). Rock and regolith consisting of a mixture of volcanic and sedimentary formations moved out of the head of the landslide, initially sliding along steeply dipping surfaces of the Philippine fault, leaving large striations known as *slickensides* parallel to the direction of movement of the slide. Below the head, or crown, of the slide, material was deposited and deformed into terraces of regolith that slid along the slip surfaces. As the rock slide reached the base of the scarp, it spread out laterally and deposited a huge fan-shaped mass of regolith that has many ridges, radial cracks, and isolated hills known as hummocks. These characteristics show that

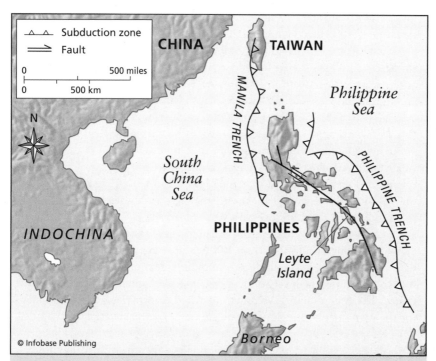

Map of Philippines landslide area, 2006. The island of Leyte is cut by a fault that has formed tall mountains that collapsed on the village of Barangay Guinsaugon on February 17, 2006, killing 1,450 people.

Rescuers search debris avalanche deposit in Leyte, Philippines, on February 18, 2006, after the avalanche buried the town of Barangay Guinsaugon, including the school that was full of children at the time. *(Landov)*

the material initially slid along fracture surfaces as a rock slide, then exploded out of the mountain as a debris avalanche that may have ridden on a cushion of air trapped beneath the falling regolith, which aided the high velocity of the flow.

The origin of the Barangay Guinsaugon landslide is uncertain, but several factors seem to have played a role. First, the active tectonics uplifted the steep mountains along the Philippine fault, and the orientation of the fault surfaces was such that many rocks were perched above loose fracture surfaces that dipped toward the open face of the mountain, with the town of Barangay Guinsaugon directly below. The landslide occurred during a period of very heavy rainfall, and the rain may have both lubricated the slip surfaces and filled open pore spaces in the regolith and rock above the slip surface, loading the slip planes beyond their ability to resist sliding. A small earthquake with a magnitude of 2.6 occurred about 15 miles (25 km) west of the head of the slide, at approximately the same time as the slide. The time of the slide is known from a telephone conversation, in which the speaker notes a loud noise, then screams in fear, and then the line went dead. It is uncertain if such a small earthquake at this distance could initiate the landslide, but the apparent coincidence is remarkable. The most likely scenario is that the steep joint surfaces were already overloaded by the weight of the new water, and the small amount of shaking from the earthquake was just enough to change a metastable slope into a moving deadly landslide. Other observations suggest that the earthquake may have occurred slightly after the landslide and may not have been a contributing cause to the disaster.

It appears that as the rock slide surged off the slopes and crashed onto the relatively flat plain below where the town was located it may have trapped a cushion of air that became compressed and surged out beneath the moving debris avalanche. This surge of air moved many houses, even a three-story concrete building, 1,800–2,000 feet (550–600 m) from where they were built and deposited them relatively intact and in the same relative positions. All the buildings that were moved in this fashion moved radially away from the source of the avalanche. Nearly all of the people who survived the debris avalanche were found along the edge of the deposit, where this cushion of air blasted structures and people from where they were and deposited them 1,800–2,000 feet (550–600 m) away.

When the landslide occurred, it buried most of the town and its residents, including the school full of 250 children and teachers. Cell phone signals and frantic text messages were received from teachers in the school, and there was tremendous hope that the students might be safe in the strong structure of the school building. The messages warned that cold waters were rapidly rising inside the school building, as the avalanche deposit became saturated with rain and river water. Rescue workers immediately focused their attention on trying to locate the site of the school beneath the rubble on the surface, consulting maps, using satellite global positioning systems (GPS), and other instruments such as ground-penetrating radar. Maps for the town were not very accurate and it was very difficult to use the radar and other instruments and rescue workers were constantly under the threat of additional landslides and had to be evacuated several times when the risk levels became too high. Still, after a couple of days, the rescue workers thought they had located the position of the school and called in heavy excavating equipment in the hope of finding survivors. Hopes were high, and high-tech sonic equipment brought in from American and Malaysian military crews that happened to be in the area detected sounds from the site. Rhythmic beating and scratching was thought to be coming from people trapped in the school. After digging frantically, the workers found no school, and the scope of the tragedy set in, with little hope of finding any additional survivors. After several weeks of surveying and analyzing data, geologists realized that the school had probably also been moved 1,650–2,000 feet (500–600 m) by the blast of compressed air from the debris avalanche and like the other buildings that were moved may have remained intact. The rescue workers were simply digging in the wrong place as the students and teachers perished. If the nature of the blast of air was better understood, perhaps rescue workers would have focused their efforts to look in the direction the school would have been moved by the blast of air preceding the debris avalanche.

Conclusion

Catastrophic downslope flows such as landslides, slumps, debris flows, lahars, and debris avalanches can be initiated by heavy rains, earthquakes, volcanic eruptions, or increases in pore pressure and loading on weak planes in the regolith and bedrock. Many of the worst landslide disasters could have been avoided if geological surveys of building sites were completed before towns and villages were located on sites of older debris flows and avalanche deposits. Other casualties from downslope flows could have been prevented if warnings were issued as lahars moved down mountain valleys or if local governments understood the lasting threats from downslope flows such as avalanches, which can release massive lahars and debris flows hours or days after the initial mass wasting event. Repetition of mass wasting events with catastrophic effects in China and Central America shows that populations generally do not remember the lessons from past disasters beyond one or two generations. It is important for local and national authorities to educate the public about natural downslope flow hazards and to enforce where towns and villages can be located in mountainous areas, to keep residents out of harm's way.

7

Reduction of Landslide Hazards and Damages

To reduce the hazards to people and property from mass wasting, it is necessary first to recognize which areas may be most susceptible to mass wasting and then to recognize the early warning signs that a catastrophic mass wasting event may be imminent. Some actions can be taken to protect people and valuable property that may be in the way of imminent downslope flows. As with many geological hazards, a past record of downslope flows is a good indicator that the area is prone to additional landslide hazards. Geological surveys and hazard assessments should be completed in mountainous and hilly terrains before construction of homes, roads, railways, power lines, and other features.

This chapter examines the specific hazards that downslope flows pose to people and property and then discusses ways that landslides and other mass wasting phenomena might be predicted and perhaps prevented. Next, methods of monitoring active downslope flows are discussed, and some basic rules about what to do in a downslope flow are listed. Finally, methods of mitigating the damage from downslope flows are discussed.

Hazards to Humans

From the descriptions of mass wasting processes and specific events above, it should be apparent that mass wasting presents a significant hazard to humans. The greatest hazards come from building on mountain slopes, which when oversteepened may fail catastrophically. The fastest-moving flows present the greatest threat to human life, with examples of the debris avalanches at Vaiont, Italy, in 1963, Nevados Huascarán, Peru, in 1962 and 1970, and the Leyte, Philippine, disaster of 2006 providing grim examples with tens of thousands of deaths. Gradual creep moves all things downhill, which accounts for the greatest cumulative amount of material moved through mass wasting events. These slow flows do not usually hurt people, but they do cause billions of dollars in damages every year. Occasionally, slow flows will accelerate into fast-moving debris flows, so it is important to monitor areas that may experience accelerated creep. Man-made structures are not designed to move downhill or to be covered in debris, so mass wasting needs to be appreciated and accounted for when designing communities, homes, roads, pipelines, etc. The best planning involves not building in areas that pose a significant hazard, but, if this cannot be done, the hazards should be minimized through slope engineering, as described below.

Prediction of Downslope Flows

What can be done to reduce the damage and human suffering inflicted by mass movements? Greater understanding of the dangers and specific triggers of mass movements can help reduce casualties from individual catastrophes, but long-term planning is needed to reduce the costs from damage to structures and infrastructure inflicted by downslope movements of all types. One approach to reducing the hazards is to produce maps that show areas that have, or are likely to suffer from, mass movements. These maps should clearly show hazard zones and areas of greatest risk from mass movements and what types of events may be expected in any given area. These maps should be made publicly available and used for planning communities, roads, pipelines, and other constructions. It is the responsibility of community planners and engineers to determine and account for these risks when building homes, roads, communities, and other parts of the nation's infrastructure.

Several factors need to be considered when making risk maps for areas prone to mass movements. First, slopes play a large role in mass movements, so anywhere there is a slope there is a potential for mass movement. In general, the steeper the slope, the greater the potential for mass movements. In addition, any undercutting or oversteepening of slopes (from coastal erosion or construction) increases the chances of downslope movements, and anything that loads the top of a slope (like a heavy building) also increases the chances of initiating a downslope flow. Slopes that are in areas prone to seismic shaking are particularly susceptible to mass flows, and the hazards are increased along these slopes. Slopes that are wet and have a buildup of water in the slope materials are well lubricated and exert extra pressure on the slope material and are thus more susceptible to failure.

The underlying geology is also a strong factor that influences whether or not a slope may fail. The presence of joints, bedding planes, or other weaknesses increases the chances of slope failure. Additionally, rocks that are soluble in water may have large open spaces, which make them more susceptible to slope failure.

Fence displaced by 1906 earthquake, near San Francisco, California *(USGS)*

These features need to be considered when preparing landslide potential maps, and, once a significant landslide potential is determined for an area, it should be avoided for building. If this is not possible, there are several choices of engineering projects that can be undertaken to reduce the risk. The slope could be engineered to remove excess water, decreasing the potential for failure. This can be accomplished through the installation of drains at the top of the slope and/or the installation of perforated pipes into the slope that help drain the excess water from the slope material, decreasing the chances of slope failure.

Prevention of Downslope Flows

Slopes can be reduced by removing material, reducing the potential for landslides. If this is not possible, the slope can be terraced, which decreases runoff and stops material from falling all the way to the base of the slope. Slopes can also be covered with stone, concrete, or other material that can reduce infiltration of water and reduce erosion of the slope material. Retaining walls can be built to hold loose material in place, and large masses of rocks can be placed along the base of the slope (called base loading), which serves to reduce the potential of the base of the slope slumping out by increasing the resistance to the movement. Unvegetated slopes can be planted, as plants and roots greatly reduce erosion, and may help soak up some of the excess water in the soil.

If a slope cannot be modified, and people must use the area, there are several other steps that may be taken to help reduce the risk. Cable nets and wire fences may be constructed around rocky slopes that are prone to rockfalls, and these wire meshes will serve to catch falling rocks before they hit passing cars or pedestrians. Large berms and ditches may be built to catch falling debris or to redirect mudflows and other earthflows. Rock sheds and tunnels may be built for shelter in areas prone to avalanches, where people can seek shelter.

Monitoring of Active Landslides

What are the signs that need to be watched for that may warn of an imminent mass wasting event? Areas that have previously suffered mass wasting events may be most prone to repeated events, so geomorphological evidence for ancient slumps and landslides should be viewed as a warning. It is recognized that seismic activity and periods of heavy rainfall destabilize slopes, and are signs of increased hazards.

Activity of springs can be monitored to detect when the slopes may be saturated and unstable, and features such as wet areas or puddles oriented parallel to an escarpment should be viewed as potential warnings that the slope is saturated and perhaps ready to slide. In some cases, slopes or whole mountains have experienced accelerated rates of creep soon before large mass wasting events, such as the Vaiont Dam disaster previously described.

The USGS, along with other local agencies, has set up some real-time monitoring programs for a few areas in California, Colorado, Washington, and New Mexico that have active landslide features. These systems include a variety of sensors that collect data in all weather conditions, then transmit this information to geological survey computers where the information is automatically processed and made accessible online to local officials, engineers, and emergency managers.

These real-time monitoring systems operate on the principle that changes from slow flows to rapid flows can be rapid and may occur during times of bad weather when residents may not be able to observe the outdoor conditions. Real-time monitoring can detect small changes in movement on ground that could be hazardous to be on, and having real-time data can be crucial in saving human lives and property. The continuous data also provides detailed information on the behavior of landslides over time that engineers can use to design controls to slow down or prevent the landslides from moving catastrophically.

Most of the systems involve monitoring of ground movements and water pressures and how these change in time. The amount and rates of downslope movement can be recorded by extensometers that can detect stretching or shortening of the ground. Extensometers are basically very sensitive instruments that can measure the distance between two points, typically across an area that is moving and one that is not. One type of extensometer would have a tube inside a pipe, with one side anchored to either side of a moving landslide slip surface. As the landslide slips or creeps, the pipes would gradually move apart, and measurements of the amount over time would give the rate of slip. More sophisticated electronic extensometers are commonly used, but operate on the same principle.

Ground vibrations or microearthquakes are also commonly monitored along active landslide features. Increases in ground vibrations can be associated with enhanced slip and movement, and geophones buried in the slides are sensitive enough to detect these small vibrations. Groundwater pressure sensors within the slides monitor the groundwater conditions within the slides, and rain gauges record precipitation. High groundwater pressures or rapid changes in groundwater pressure can indicate that the landslide is on the verge of accelerated slip.

The real-time monitoring systems currently in use normally transmit data to the USGS every 10 minutes. If there is strong ground motion or other indications of an imminent slide, the data is transmitted immediately, and warnings can be issued to areas at risk. Sites currently being monitored include several in the Northern California Coast Ranges and in the Sierra Nevada, in Washington State near Seattle, in New Mexico, and in several places prone to slow landslides and rapid avalanches in Colorado. Active ground movement is occurring in every state in the country, and it is hoped that real-time monitoring programs can be extended to many other active and potentially hazardous sites. There are precautions, which will save lives during landslide events, as explained in the following sidebar on what to do in a downslope flow.

Mitigation of Damages from Downslope Flows

Once a landslide has occurred it is difficult to recover property losses. Some areas in California were once very expensive ocean-view real estate, but once large slumps started moving whole neighborhoods downslope along systems of curved faults, the properties became worthless. The best way to avoid financial and property loss in places like this is not to rebuild, as once the land slips in these regions it takes huge engineering efforts to prevent further movements. Sometimes the only way to prevent additional landslides is to completely reengineer the slopes, changing steep slopes into terraced low-angle hills. Even this type of engineering may not be enough to prevent additional slides, so the best protection is to avoid building on land that has a history of sliding.

Despite these cautions, many new developments in landslide mitigation techniques make living in mountainous or hilly terrain safer. Most early landslide repair and mitigation techniques involved the building and emplacement of buttresses along the toes of landslides to stop their forward advance and emplacement of pipes and other features to promote water drainage from within the slides. Later, in the mid-20th century, as equipment for moving regolith became larger, it became more common to remove entire slide masses from the sides of hillsides and to recompact the material to stabilize the slopes. Since the 1990s, new products such as geomembranes and geotextiles that can hold regolith

WHAT TO DO IN A DOWNSLOPE FLOW

Residents of areas prone to landslides or other mass wasting movements need to keep an eye on their surroundings and watch for falling rocks, debris, and sliding slopes. If authorities warn of an imminent slope failure, then residents should leave immediately. Many downslope flows begin as slow movements, then accelerate into dangerous flows. If the early warning signs of trouble are heeded, lives can be saved. Anyone who sees a rapid downslope flow moving toward them may have only a few seconds or minutes to respond and get to higher ground. In many places prone to avalanches, civic authorities have constructed avalanche shelters designed to withstand the force of the avalanche. Lives have been saved by observant people ushering others into one of these structures during an avalanche, where people are safe and authorities know where to search for survivors.

The USGS has issued an eight-point bulletin about things to do to reduce landslide risks for people who live near steep hills. Prior to intense storms the following is recommended:

- Become familiar with the surrounding land. Determine if there is a past history of debris flows in the region by contacting local officials, geological surveys, or university geology departments. Slopes where debris flows have occurred in the past are likely to experience them again.
- Support local government efforts to develop and enforce land use and building ordinances that regulate construction in areas prone to landslides and debris flows. Buildings need to be located away from streams and rivers, steep slopes, and the mouths of mountain channels.
- Watch the patterns of storm water drainage on slopes near homes, noting where water converges and increases flow over soil-covered slopes. These areas could be more susceptible to landslides. Check the hillsides for any signs of land movement, including small landslides or debris flows, tilted trees and poles, bent features, or elongate and curved gullies parallel to the slope.
- Determine the emergency response and evacuation plans that may be in place with local authorities and have backup plans for family and businesses.

In addition to these preparations, it is good to know what to do during intense storms, when landslides and other downslope flows are most likely to occur. The USGS recommends the following:

- Stay alert and awake. Many debris flow fatalities occur when people are sleeping. Listen for warnings on the radio and be especially alert during short very intense rainfalls after prolonged periods of rain.
- Consider leaving areas that are particularly hazardous, areas near steep slopes, areas that have had previous landslides, or areas near mouths of mountain valleys.
- Be alert for any unusual sounds that could indicate moving ground and debris. Sounds of cracking trees, boulders banging together, or trembling ground are particularly grave warnings that could indicate a large landslide moving downhill. Small trickles of flowing or falling mud may precede larger flows and any sudden increase or decrease in water flow patterns or a change from clear water to muddy water should be taken as warnings that a landslide could be imminent. With any of these warnings it is best to leave dangerous areas immediately.
- Evacuating dangerous areas can also be dangerous. Embankments along roads are very prone to landslides during heavy rains, so care must be taken to avoid landslides, debris flows, falling rocks, and debris while in mountainous terrain.

in place and allow water to escape have greatly increased the ability to stabilize slopes to make them safer from sliding.

The beginning of slope reengineering to prevent or mitigate landslides is thought to have started in the early 1830s, along railroad lines in England and France. With the Industrial Revolution in the late 1800s, engineers used steam engines to excavate slopes to 1:1 (horizontal to vertical) or a 45-degree slope. Steeper slopes were covered with masonry retaining walls, holding the slopes back with gravity. When slopes failed in downslope movements, they were typically repaired by cutting the slope back to more gentle slopes, or, if space in urban areas did not permit this, the slopes were reinforced with concrete or masonry walls.

After World War II, large earthwork projects were started in the United States, particularly associated with the Interstate Highway Act of 1955. At this time, a new style of landslide mitigation became common, that of excavating the entire slipped area, installing subdrainages, then refilling and compacting the slopes with the excavated material. These so-called buttress fills are still the most common form of landslide repair in the United States and are moderately effective in most cases. Slopes can be modified, slip surfaces removed, and the subdrainages keep pore water pressures to a minimum.

Since the 1990s, new materials have been developed that help engineers mitigate the effects of landslides and reduce the risks of additional slope failures on repaired slopes. These materials are known as geosynthetics and geomembrane materials and include many individual types of construction and materials. Pavement cloths are tack-coated membranes that are overlain on existing pavement, then paved over. They serve to hold the pavement together but allow water to escape through the membrane. Filter cloths are used beneath roads and railroad ballast and on hillsides to prevent settlement of gravels into the underlying soils. They help to stabilize slopes and prevent hillside drains and other embankments from settling. Liner membranes are impervious to water and can be used to isolate areas of contaminated or clean groundwater from regional groundwater systems. Drainage membranes are constructed as composites of these materials and can be used in the construction of retaining walls, combining different effects of not allowing water in some places and forcing water to drain in others that are less hazardous. Other materials, known as geogrids, can be stretched across slopes, and these materials add strength and support to toes of slopes that might otherwise collapse.

Slope stabilization by a retaining wall along a coastal highway in Spain *(Alamy)*

Since the 1960s, soils on slopes have been engineered by mixing materials into the soil so that they have additional strength, much like the natural effect of having abundant roots in soil. These reinforced earth walls have become common along highways and above retaining walls. In other cases, strong materials are partly buried along the toes of slides or bases of slopes that could potentially fail. These reinforcements are typically designed as grids, increasing the strength of the toe of the slopes so that they are less susceptible to failure. These grids are typically extended into the slope for a distance of about 1.5 times the slope height. In addition, the surfaces of faces of the slopes are wrapped with the reinforcement grids, and then the surface between the grids is planted, further promoting slope stability.

Conclusion

Slopes present dangers to people and property when they fail in landslides and other downslope flows. The likelihood of a landslide or other mass wasting event occurring in any area can be predicted by knowing the history of past downslope flows in the area, and the most hazardous areas should be avoided for development. Slopes can be modified and reinforced to reduce the likelihood of a landslide, and real-time monitoring and warning systems have been installed in a few locations with active landsliding in the United States. Warning signs, such as increases in mudflows or trees and boulders moving downhill, should be heeded as an extremely urgent sign that a rapid avalanche may be about to occur. Once a landslide does occur, it is difficult to further stabilize the slope. However, recent techniques of removing large amounts of material from hillsides, installing sub-slide drainage, replacing and recompacting the slide material, and installing grids of material that strengthen the slope can make hillsides relatively safe.

Summary

The outermost layer of the Earth consists of an assortment of loose soil, rocks, organic material, and partially altered bedrock that is collectively known as regolith. Most interactions between people and Earth's materials involve this regolith, and this book has examined many of the hazardous aspects of this regolith. There are sections on weathering and the formation of soils and concentration of harmful elements within soils, then a section on the hazards of harmful gases and contaminated waters in the soil and regolith. Processes of mass wasting, where soil and rock of the regolith move downhill, were classified and discussed with the specific hazards of different types of flows presented. Case examples of some of the worst disasters from different kinds of downslope flows were presented. Next, some recommendations about what to do during mass wasting events were listed, with an overview of different techniques to predict, prevent, and mitigate the damages from downslope flows also presented.

The formation of soils from bedrock involves the chemical, mechanical, and biological breakdown of the bedrock into its weathered products. In most cases, the soluble material is leached away by water and the remaining soil contains concentrations of the unsoluble materials such as aluminum, iron, and silica. Variations in climate lead to variations in which processes dominate the transition from bedrock to soil and lead to differences in the types of soils developed. These natural processes have in some cases concentrated hazardous elements in soils. Some of the more significant harmful elements that tend to get concentrated in soils and the regolith include selenium and iodine. Shallow mining can expose people to harmful levels of asbestos, lead, silica, and coal dust. Radon gas poses significant hazards to much of the United States and moves silently into homes, where it can be inhaled, leading to health problems. However, this hazard is easily mitigated, and homes can be made safe from radon at relatively low expense.

The regolith contains vast quantities of groundwater, amounting to about 35 times the amount of all the freshwater in surface lakes and streams. This water is a vital resource and is threatened in many places by pollution, depletion, and contamination by natural hazardous elements from the regolith. In some parts of the world, arsenic is so concentrated in groundwaters that it has caused a range of diseases in local populations, including many cases of hyperkeratosis and several types of cancer. Water in the regolith also significantly changes the mechanical properties of the soils. Some clay-rich soils expand and contract by 25–50 percent when they are wet, and these expansive soils cause billions of dollars worth of damage to structures every year in the United States alone. Engineers need to deal with a range of changing physical properties of soils that alter with the addition of water.

Mass wasting is the movement of soil, regolith, or rock downhill without the direct aid of water. Gravity is the main driving force of mass wasting, pulling material downslope at rates that range from imperceptible to hundreds of MPH. Different types of mass wasting flows, together called landslides, can be classified based on the rate at which they move, the material that moves (whether it is rock, regolith, or pure soil), and the amount of water mixed with the regolith. Most places in the world and every state in the United States experience some kind of mass wasting. The slow movements such as creep do the most economic damage, costing billions of dollars a year in the United States. Fast movements have proven the most catastrophic in terms of lost lives, with some examples killing tens of thousands of people in individual events. Submarine mass wasting also poses a significant threat to people, mostly in that large submarine slides can generate tsunamis that hit otherwise peaceful shorelines, potentially killing huge numbers of people.

The hazards to humans of downslope flows include economic losses and the danger from deadly debris avalanches and mudflows in mountainous areas. Residents of these areas should know not to build on top of older landslide, mudflow, and avalanche deposits. In periods of heavy rainfall, residents need to keep an alert eye out for signs of an impending landslide, such as streams suddenly becoming muddy or the land surface slowly moving at progressively more rapid rates. Once landslides do occur, it is best to avoid future building on the slipped ground, since it is likely to move again. However, recent developments in geoengineering have improved the ability to modify slipped slopes so that they are relatively safe and usable with proper monitoring systems set in place.

Glossary

abyssal plains—Large flat areas that cover much of the ocean floor. They are typically covered with fine-grained sedimentary deposits called deep-sea oozes, derived from the small skeletons of siliceous organisms that fell to the seafloor.

age elements—Elements that tend to accumulate in tissues as they get older.

angle of repose—The steepest angle that a loose material such as sand, gravel, or boulders can be stacked at.

aquifers—Any body of permeable rock or regolith saturated with water through which groundwater moves.

artesian system—A groundwater system in which the water is confined to a certain layer, and pressure at depth is high enough to cause the water to rise along a fracture or artificial hole such as a well. The pressure is usually caused by the aquifer layer being tilted so that it is at higher elevation in nearby mountains, and the weight of the water in the confined layer causes it to rise along the fracture or well at a lower elevation.

avalanche—A moving mixture of rock, soil, or regolith that moves rapidly, perhaps by riding on a cushion of air trapped as the material fell off a nearby mountain.

biological weathering—The breaking down of rocks and minerals by biological agents.

caldera—A roughly circular or elliptical depression, often occupied by a lake, that forms when the rocks above a subterranean magma mass collapse into the magma during a cataclysmic eruption.

chemical weathering—Decomposition of rocks through the alteration of individual mineral grains.

continental shelf—Generally flat areas on the edges of continents, underlain by continental crust and having shallow water. Sedimentary deposits on continental shelves include muds, sands, and carbonates.

convergent plate boundaries—Places where two plates move toward each other, resulting in one plate sliding beneath the other when a dense oceanic plate is involved, or collision and deformation, when continental plates are involved. These types of plate boundaries may have the largest of all earthquakes.

corrosiveness—In soil, a measure of the ability to corrode or chemically decompose buried objects, such as pipes, wires, tanks, and posts.

creep—The imperceptible slow downslope flowing movement of regolith involving the very slow plastic deformation of the regolith, as well as repeated microfracturing of bedrock at nearly imperceptible rates.

debris avalanche—A granular flow moving at very high velocity and covering large distances.

debris flow—The downslope movement of unconsolidated regolith, most of which is coarser than sand and typically chaotically mixed between fragments of different sizes. Some debris flows begin as slumps, but then continue to flow downhill as debris flows. They typically fan out and come to rest when they emerge out of steeply sloping mountain valleys onto flatter plains.

dike—Any tablular, parallel-sided igneous intrusion that generally cuts across layering in the surrounding country rocks.

downslope flow—Movement of a sediment/water/rock mixture downhill.

earthflow—A generally slow-moving downslope flow that forms on moderate slopes with adequate moisture and develops preferentially in fine-grained deformable soils such as clays, as well as rocky soils that have a silt or clay matrix. Earthflows can contribute large amounts of sediment to streams and rivers and typically move in short periods of episodic movement or relatively steady movement in response to heavy rainfall events, earthquakes, irrigations, or other disturbances. Most earthflows move along a basal shear surface and are characterized by internal deformation of the sliding material and do not fail catastrophically but do cause significant damage to infrastructure.

earthquake—A sudden release of energy from a slip on a fault, an explosion, or other event that causes the ground to shake and vibrate, associated with the passage of waves of energy released at its source. An earthquake originates in one place and then spreads out in all directions along the fault plane.

exfoliation—A weathering process where rocks spall off in successive shells, like the skin of an onion. Exfoliation is caused by differential stresses within a rock formed during chemical weathering processes.

expansive soils—Soils that add layers of water molecules between the plates of clay minerals (made of silica, aluminum, and oxygen), loosely bonding the water in the mineral, and are capable of expanding by up to 50 percent more than their dry volume.

falls—In mass wasting, when regolith moves freely through the air and lands at the base of a slope or escarpment.

flows—In mass wasting, movements of regolith, rock, water, and air in which the moving mass breaks into many pieces that flow in a chaotic mass movement.

granite—Common igneous rock in the continental crust. Granite contains quartz and the volcanic or extrusive equivalent of granite is rhyolite.

granular flow—A downslope flow in which the full weight of the flowing sediment is supported by grain-to-grain contact between individual grains.

groundwater—All the water contained within spaces in bedrock, soil, and regolith.

hot spot—An area of unusually active magmatic activity that is not associated with a plate boundary. Hot spots are thought to form above a plume of magma rising from deep in the mantle.

humus—Partially decomposed organic material in soil.

hydrolysis—A chemical reaction involving the decomposition of water. In geology, hydrolysis reactions are typically between silicate minerals and water, consuming either H^+ or OH^- ions, and thus changing the H^+/OH^- ratio.

igneous rocks—Rocks that have crystallized from a molten state known as magma. These include plutonic rocks, crystallized below the surface, and volcanic rocks, that have crystallized at the surface.

joints—Small fractures in rocks across which there is no observable displacement.

lahar—A mudflow formed by the mixture of volcanic ash and water. Lahars are common on volcanoes, both during and for years after major eruptions.

landslide—A general name for any downslope movement of a mass of bedrock, regolith, or a mixture of rock and soil, commonly used to indicate any mass wasting process.

lava—Magma, or molten rock, that flows at the surface of the Earth.

liquefaction—A process where sudden shaking of certain types of water-saturated sands and muds turns these once-solid sediments into a slurry with a liquid consistency.

lithosphere—Rigid outer shell of the Earth that is about 75 miles (125 km) thick under continents and 45 miles (75 km) thick under oceans. The basic theorem of plate tectonics is that the lithosphere of the Earth is broken into about 12 large rigid blocks or plates that are all moving relative to one another.

loess—Fine-grained windblown dust.

mass wasting—The movement of material downhill without the direct involvement of water.

mechanical weathering—The disintegration of rocks, generally by abrasion.

medical geology—An emerging science that studies the effects of geological materials, processes, and trace elements in the environment on human and animal health.

mudflow—A downslope flow that resembles a debris flow except that it has a higher concentration of water (up to 30 percent), which makes it more fluid, with a consistency ranging from soup to wet concrete. Mudflows often start as muddy streams in dry mountain canyons, which pick up more and more mud and sand as they move, until eventually the front of the stream is a wall of moving mud and rock.

passive margin—A boundary between continental and oceanic crust that is not a plate boundary, characterized by thick deposits of sedimentary rocks. These margins typically have a flat, shallow water shelf, then a steep drop-off to deep ocean floor rocks away from the continent.

permeability—A body's capacity to transmit fluids or to allow the fluids to move through its open pore spaces.

plate tectonics—A model that describes the process related to the slow motions of more than a dozen rigid plates of solid rock around the surface of the Earth. The plates ride on a deeper layer of partially molten material that is found at depths starting at 60–200 miles (100–320 km) beneath the surface of the continents and 1–100 miles (1–160 km) beneath the oceans.

Plinian—A type of volcanic eruption characterized by a large and tall eruption column, typically reaching tens of thousands of feet into the air. Named after Pliny the Elder, from his description of Vesuvius.

porosity—The percentage of total volume of a body that consists of open spaces.

pyroclastic—A general term for rocks and material that are thrown from a volcano, including the explosive ash, bombs, and parts of the volcano ripped off the slopes during eruptions.

radon—A poisonous gas produced as a product of the radioactive decay product of the uranium decay series. Radon is a heavy gas, and it presents a serious indoor health hazard in every part of the country.

regolith—The outer surface layer of the Earth, consisting of a mixture of soil, organic material, and partially weathered bedrock.

rockfall—Free fall of detached bodies of bedrock from a cliff or steep slope.

rock slide—The sudden downslope movement of newly detached masses of bedrock (or debris slides, if the rocks are mixed with other material or regolith).

sediment flow—Mass wasting processes that involve flow are transitional within themselves and to stream-type flows in the amounts of sediment/water they contain and in velocity. There are many names for the different types of sediment flows, including slurry flows, mudflows, debris flows, debris avalanches, earthflow, and loess flow.

sensitivity—In soil, a measure of how the strength changes with shaking or with other disturbances such as those associated with excavation or construction.

shrink/swell potential—In soil, a measure of a soil's ability to add or lose water at a molecular level.

sinkholes—Generally semicircular depressions found in karst terrains where groundwater dissolution of underlying rocks is common. Sinkholes have subterranean drainage and may form by the collapse of underground caves.

slickenlines—Striations along fault surfaces that form by the scratching and movement of one block of rock or regolith against the other. The slickenline striations are oriented parallel to the direction of movement along the fault.

slickenside—A fault surface containing scratches, striations, or fibers known as slickenlines that are oriented parallel to the fault movement direction.

slides—In mass wasting, when rock, soil, water, and debris move over and in contact with the underlying surface.

slump—A type of mass wasting where a large mass of rock or sediment moves downward and outward along an upward curving fault surface. Slumps may occur under the sea or on the land.

slurry flow—A moving mass of sediment saturated in water that is transported with the flowing mass. The mixture is so dense that it can suspend large boulders or roll them along the base.

soil profile—A succession of distinctive horizons in a soil from the surface downward to unaltered bedrock.

solifluction—The slow viscous downslope movement of waterlogged soil and debris. Solifluction is most common in polar latitudes where the top layer of permafrost melts, resulting in a water-saturated mixture resting on a frozen base.

spheroidal weathering—A weathering process that proceeds along two or more sets of joints in the subsurface, resulting in shells of weathered rock that surround unaltered rocks, looking like boulders.

springs—Places where groundwater flows out at the ground surface.

subsidence—Sinking of one surface, such as the land, relative to another surface, such as sea level.

Superfund site—A hazardous waste site designated as eligible for being cleaned up using special funds allocated by the U.S. Environmental Protection Agency.

talus—The entire body of rock waste sloping away from the mountains; the sediments composing it is known as sliderock. This rock debris accumulates at the bases of mountain slopes, deposited there by rockfalls, slides, and other downslope movements.

translational slide—A variation of a slump in which the sliding mass moves not on a curved surface, but downslope on a preexisting plane, such as a weak bedding plane or a joint. Translational slides may remain relatively coherent or break into small blocks forming a debris slide.

tsunami—A giant harbor or deepwater wave, with long wavelengths, initiated by submarine landslides, earthquakes, volcanic eruptions, or other causes that suddenly displace large amounts of water. Tsunamis can be much larger than normal waves when they strike the shore and cause great damage and destruction.

turbidity current—Subaqueous downslope flow of water-saturated sand and mud that leaves behind a turbidite deposit of graded sand and shale.

Further Reading and Web Sites

BOOKS

Alley, W. M., T. E. Reilly, and O. L. Franke. *Sustainability of Ground-Water Resources.* United States Geological Survey Circular 1186, 1999. This book discusses the use and misuse of groundwater, including the effects of contamination and pollution.

Armstrong, B. R., and K. Williams. *The Avalanche Book.* Armstrong, Colo.: Fulcrum Publishing, 1992. This is a comprehensive and readable book about avalanches and their hazards.

Birkland, P. W. *Soils and Geomorphology.* New York: Oxford University Press, 1984. This is a general, college-level textbook on soil science and geomorphology.

Brabb, E. E., and B. L. Harrod. *Landslides: Extent and Economic Significance.* Proceedings of the 28th International Geological Congress: Symposium on Landslides, Washington, D.C., July 17, 1989. Rotterdam: A. A. Balkema, 1989. This technical book contains a series of separate papers on the abundance and economic significance of landslides in many countries and regions of the world.

Bucknam, Robert C., Jeffrey A. Coe, Manuel Mota Chavarria, Jonathan W. Godt, Arthur C. Tarr, Lee-Ann Bradley, Sharon Rafferty, Dean Hancock, Richard L. Dart, and Margo L. Johnson. *Landslides Triggered by Hurricane Mitch in Guatemala—Inventory and Discussion.* United States Geological Survey open-file report 01-0443, 2001. A review and inventory of the landslides produced by the heavy rains of Hurricane Mitch in Guatemala.

Cannon, Susan H., Kathleen M. Haller, Ingrid Ekstrom, Eugene S. Schweig III, Graziella Devoli, David W. Moore, Sharon A. Rafferty, and Arthur C. Tarr. *Landslide Response to Hurricane Mitch Rainfall in Seven Study Areas in Nicaragua.* United States Geological Survey open-file report 01-0412A, 2001. A review and inventory of the landslides produced by the heavy rains of Hurricane Mitch in Nicaragua.

Clark, J. W., W. Viessman, Jr., and M. J. Hammer. *Water Supply and Pol-*

lution Control. New York: Harper and Row, 1977. This is a general college-level textbook on water supply issues, with many tables and statistics.

Coates, D. R., ed. "Landslides," *Geological Society of America Reviews in Engineering Geology* 3, 1977. This book contains a review of methods to mitigate the damages from landslides prior to the middle 1970s.

Cothern, C. R., and J. E. Smith, Jr. *Environmental Radon.* New York: Plenum Publishing Corp., 1987. This source discusses the geology and environmental consequences of radon.

Crone, Anthony J., Rex L. Baum, David J. Lidke, Damon N. D. Sather, Lee-Ann Bradley, and Arthur C. Tarr. *Landslides Induced by Hurricane Mitch in El Salvador—An Inventory and Descriptions of Selected Features.* United States Geological Survey open-file report 01-0444, 2001. A review and inventory of the landslides produced by the heavy rains of Hurricane Mitch in El Salvador.

Jones, F. O. *Landslides in Rio de Janeiro and the Serra das Araras escarpment, Brazil.* United States Geological Survey Professional Paper 697, Washington, D.C., U.S. Government Printing Office, 1973. This book describes landslides in the Rio de Janeiro area of Brazil.

Kusky, T. M. *Geologic Hazards, A Sourcebook.* Westport, Conn.: Greenwood Press, 2002. This introductory text offers descriptions of many geologic hazards including landslides.

———. *Encyclopedia of Earth Science.* New York: Facts On File, 2005. This encyclopedia contains 700 entries with definitions and descriptions of many geologic phenomena and is extensively illustrated and cross referenced. Good for college and high school levels.

Matthews, W. H., and K. C. McTaggert. Hope rockslides, British Columbia, in B. Voight, ed *Rockslides and Avalanches.* Amsterdam: Elsevier, 1978. This book contains technical descriptions of rockslides and avalanches with numerous examples, including the deadly Hope rockslide in Canada.

Mileti, D. S., P. A. Bolton, G. Fernandez, and R. G. Updike. *The eruption of Nevado del Ruiz Volcano, Colombia, South America, November 13, 1985.* Committee on Natural Disasters, National Research Council, Natural Disaster Studies, 4:109 p., Washington, D.C.: National Academy Press, 1991. This book describes the eruption of Nevado del Ruiz in 1985 and the devastating mudslides that flowed into surrounding valleys.

Nazaroff, W. W., and A. V. Nero, Jr., eds. *Radon and Its Decay Products in Indoor Air.* New York: John Wiley and Sons, 1988. This textbook describes the radioactive decay series from radon to polonium, and how polonium is a health risk to humans when it is trapped in lung tissue.

Nilsen, T. H., and E. E. Brabb. *Landslides,* in R. D. Borcherdt, ed., *Studies for Seismic Zonation of the San Francisco Bay Region,* USGS Professional Paper 941A, 1975. The report examines the history and potential for landslides in the San Francisco Bay Area.

Otton, J. K., L. C. S. Gundersen, and R. R. Schumann. *The Geology of Radon.* USGS, General Interest Publication 1993–0-356–733, 1993. This short pamphlet is a readable discussion of where radon is concentrated, how it enters homes, and the ill health effects it can cause.

Plafker, G., and G. E. Ericksen. "Nevados Huascarán avalanches, Peru," chapter 8 in Voight, B., ed. *Rockslides and Avalanches.* Amsterdam: Elsevier, 1978. This chapter presents a detailed description and analysis of the Nevados Huascarán disasters in South America.

Ross, M. "The Health Effects of Mineral Dusts," in *The Environmental Geochemistry of Mineral Deposits, Part A: Processes, Techniques, and Health Issues.* Society of Economic Geologists, Reviews in Economic Geology 6A, 1999. This is a technical review of where hazardous minerals may be located and the health risks they pose.

Schultz, A. P., and C. S. Southworth, eds. *Landslides in Eastern North America.* USGS Circular 1008, 1987. This technical report provides many maps and examples of landslide deposits from the Appalachians and eastern North America.

Schuster, R. L. "The 25 most catastrophic landslides of the 20th century," in Chacon, Irigaray, and Fernandez, eds. *Landslides,* proceedings of the 8th International Conference & Field Trip on Landslides, Granada, Spain, 27–28 September, 1966. Rotterdam: Balkema, 1966. Although premature, this book describes the most disastrous 20th-century landslides that occurred prior to 1965.

Terzaghi, K. "Mechanism of landslides," in Berkey, C., ed. *Applications of Geology to Engineering Practice.* New York: Geological Society of America, 1950. This is a now-classic treatise on how landslides work.

U.S. EPA. *Home Buyer's and Seller's Guide to Radon.* EPA 402-R-93–003, 1993. A general booklet on what to do about radon when buying or selling a home.

———. *Consumer's Guide to Radon Reduction: How to Reduce Radon Levels in Your Home.* EPA 402-K92–003, 1992. A general interest booklet about how to reduce the level of radon in homes that test positive for radon.

United States Environmental Protection Agency and Centers for Disease Control. *A Citizen's Guide to Radon: The Guide to Protecting Yourself and Your Family from Radon.* 2nd ed. EPA 402-K92–001, 1992. A general interest booklet on how to check for and reduce the risk of radon in homes and the environment.

United States Geological Survey. "The Alaska Earthquake, March 27, 1964." *Geological Survey Professional Papers* 542-B "Effects on Communities-

Whittier"; 542-D "Effects on Communities- Homer"; 542-E "Effects on Communities, Seward"; 542-G "Effects on Communities-Various Communities"; 543-A "Regional Effects; Slide-induced waves, seiching and ground fracturing at Kenai Lake"; 543-1 "Regional Effects- Tectonics"; 543-B "Regional Effects- Martin-Bering Rivers area"; 543-F "Regional Effects- Ground Breakage in the Cook Inlet area"; 543-H "Regional Effects- Erosion and Deposition on a Raised Beach, Montague Island"; 543-J "Regional Effects; Shore Processes and Beach Morphology"; 544-C "Effects on Hydrologic Regime- Outside Alaska"; 544-D "Effects on Hydrologic Regime–Glaciers"; 544-E "Effects on Hydrologic Regime-Seismic Seiches"; 545-A "Effects on Transportation and Utilities- Eklutna Power Project," Menlo Park: U.S. Geological Survey, 1966. This series of reports describes landslides and other effects of the 1964 Alaskan earthquake.

Varnes, D. J. "Slope movement types and processes," in R. L. Schuster and R. J. Krizek, eds. *Landslides, Analysis and Control.* Washington D.C.: National Academy of Sciences, 1978. This chapter in this technical book describes ways to reduce the damage from downslope flows.

West, T. R. *Geology Applied to Engineering.* Englewood Cliffs, N.J.: Prentice Hall, 1995. This textbook provides geological background to engineers, especially in the area of slope stability.

JOURNAL ARTICLES

Close, U., and McCormick. "Where the Mountains Walked." *National Geographic Magazine* 41, 1922. This is a classic general interest article about evidence for mass wasting processes on mountain slopes.

Cluff, L. S. "Peru Earthquake of May 31, 1970; Engineering Geology Observations." *Seismological Society of America Bulletin* 61, 1971. This technical article discusses the responses of different types of buildings and soils to the massive Peru earthquake of 1970.

Finkelman, R. B., H. C. Skinner, G. S. Plumlee, and J. E. Bunnell. "Medical Geology," *Geotimes,* 2001. This article describes the emerging science of medical geology, how natural elements and processes affect human health.

Gates, A. E., and L. C. S. Gundersen, eds. "Geologic Controls on Radon." *Geological Society of America* Special Paper 271, 1992, 88 pp. This article describes why radon is concentrated in some places and not in other places.

Goldsmith, D. F. "Health Effects of Silica Dust Exposure." *Silica: Physical Behavior, Geochemistry and Materials Applications, Reviews in Mineralogy* 29, 1994. This review article presents the science behind the human health risks of exposure to silica dust.

Hsu, K. J. "Catastrophic debris streams (sturzstroms) generated by rockfalls." *Geological Society of America Bulletin* 86, 1989. Describes a special class of debris flows derived from rockfalls.

Hubbert, M. K., and W. W. Rubey. "Role of fluid pressure in mechanics of overthrust faulting: I. Mechanics of fluid-filled porous solids and its application to overthrust faulting. *Geological Society of America Bulletin* 70, 1959. This classic paper describes the role of fluids in lubricating faults and is the source of the famous "beer can" experiment.

Kiersch, G. A. "Vaiont reservoir disaster." *Civil Engineering,* 1964. This presents a description of the mechanical properties of the mountains that collapsed leading to the Vaiont reservoir disaster.

Lagmay, A. M. A., T. O. Burtkenley, T. Ong, and D. Ferdinand. "Scientists investigate recent Philippine landslide." *EOS* 87, 2006. This technical news report describes the first scientific investigation of the massive landslide on Leyte Island, Philippines, on February 17, 2006.

Morales, B. "The Huascarán avalanche in the Santa Valley, Peru." In *Proceedings, International Symposium on Scientific Aspects of Snow and Ice Avalanches,* 5–10 April 1965. Davos, Switzerland: International Association of Scientific Hydrology Publication No. 69, 1966. This technical paper describes the 1962 debris avalanche from Nevados Huscarán in Peru that buried the village of Ranrahirca, killing 4,000–5,000 people.

Muller, L. "The rock slide in the Vaiont Valley." *Rock Mechanics and Engineering Geology* 2, 1968. In this technical report, the conditions that led to the large rock slide in the Vaiont Valley of northern Italy are described and the warning signs that a huge mass wasting event was about to occur are discussed.

Mutamansky, J. M. "The War on Black Lung." *Earth and Mineral Sciences* 59, 1990. This article discusses the battle to protect miners from black lung disease.

Norris, R. M. "Sea Cliff Erosion." *Geotimes* 35, 1990. Many examples of sea cliff erosion are shown in this general interest paper, and people's efforts to slow the collapse of coastal cliffs in California and other places are discussed.

Pinter, N., and M. Brandon. "How erosion builds mountains." *Scientific American, Earth from the Inside Out,* edited by J. Rennie, 2000. The interplay between erosion, formation of steep topography, and uplift of mountains is discussed in this general interest paper.

Plafker, G., Ericksen, G. E., and J. Fernandez Concha. "Geological aspects of the May 31, 1979, Peru earthquake." *Seismological Society of America Bulletin* 61, 1971. This technical paper describes the tectonic setting and regional geology of the area affected by the 1979 Peruvian earthquake.

Revkin, A. C. "Sunken Fires Menace Land and Climate." *New York Times,* January 15, 2002. This newspaper article about gases from underground fires, especially in China, emitting more carbon dioxide to the atmosphere than all the cars and trucks in the United States, presenting a major risk to global climate.

Schuster, R. L. "Landslides and floods triggered by the June 6, 1994, Paez earthquake, southwestern Colombia." *Association of Engineering Geologists, AEG News* 38, 1995. This news report described numerous landslides and floods that were initiated by the 1994 Paez earthquake in Colombia.

———, and R. W. Fleming. "Economic losses and fatalities due to landslides." *Bulletin of the Association of Engineering Geologists* 23, 1986. This article examines the statistics associated with loss of life and property and productivity from landslides.

Schuster, R. L., A. S. Nieto, T. D. O'Rourke, E. Crespo, and G. Plaza-Nieto. "Mass wasting triggered by the 5 March 1987 Ecuador earthquakes." *Engineering Geology.* Amsterdam: Elsevier, 1995. This article makes an inventory and described the different landslides and related phenomena that hit parts of Ecuador during the 1987 earthquakes.

Shaefer, S. J., and S. N. Williams. "Landslide Hazards." *Geotimes* 36, 1991. This is a nontechnical review of the different types of hazards posed by different types of mass wasting events.

Voight, B. "The Nevado del Ruiz volcano catastrophe; anatomy and retrospection." *Journal of Volcanology and Geothermal Resources* 44, 1990. The mudflows that were triggered by the eruption of Nevado del Ruiz volcano in 1985, killing 20,000 people, are described in this report.

———, R. J. Janda, H. Glicken, and P. M. Douglass. "Nature and mechanisms of the Mount Saint Helens rockslide avalanche of 18 May 1980." *Geotechnique* 33, 1983. The massive lateral blast and rockslide from the 1980 eruption of Mount Saint Helens volcano are described in this technical report.

Wilgoren, J. "100 Families Leaving Tainted Town for Cleanup." *New York Times,* January 19, 2002. This article describes the clean up of Herculaneum, Missouri, from the lead dust emitted from the Doe Run lead smelter.

INTERNET RESOURCES

In the past few years numerous Web sites with information about landslides, mass wastings, and soil and mineral hazards have appeared. Most of these Web sites are free and include historical information about specific hazards and disasters, real-time monitoring of active landslides around the world, and educational material. The sites listed below have interesting information, statistics, and graphics about these hazards. This book may serve as a useful companion while surfing through the information on the internet when encountering unfamiliar phrases, terms, or concepts that are not fully explained on the Web site. The following list of Web sites is recommended to help enrich the content of this book and make your exploration of landslides, mass wasting, and soil and mineral hazards more enjoyable. In addition, any landslides that occur after this book goes to press will be discussed on these Web sites, so checking them can help you keep this book up to date. From these Web sites you will also be able to link to a large variety of hazard-related sites. Every effort has been made to ensure the accuracy of the information provided for these Web sites. However, due to the dynamic nature of the internet, changes might occur, and any inconvenience is regretted.

Federal Emergency Management Agency. Available online. URL: http://www.fema.gov. Accessed May 23, 2007. FEMA is the nation's premier agency for emergency management and preparation. It issues warnings and evacuation orders when disasters appear imminent. FEMA maintains a Web site that is updated at least daily, includes information of hurricanes, floods, fires, national flood insurance, and information on disaster prevention, preparation, and emergency management. Divided into national and regional sites. Also contains information on costs of disasters, maps, and directions on how to do business with FEMA.

National Aeronautic and Space Administration. Available online. URL: http://earthobservatory.nasa.gov/NaturalHazards/. Accessed May 23, 2007. NASA's Web site on Natural Hazards: Earth scientists around the world use NASA satellite imagery to better understand the causes and effects of natural hazards. This site posts many public domain images to help people visualize where and when natural hazards occur and to help mitigate their effects. All images in this section are freely available to the public for reuse or republication.

National Oceanographic and Atmospheric Administration, hazards research. Available online. URL: http://ngdc.noaa.gov/seg/hazard/tsu.html. Accessed March 28, 2007. Web site about hazards, including landslides.

Natural Hazards Observer. Available online. URL: http://www.colorado.edu/hazards/o/. Accessed May 23, 2007. This Web site is the online version of the periodical, *Natural Hazards Observer. Natural Hazards Observer* is the bimonthly periodical of the Natural Hazards Center. It covers current disaster issues; new international, national, and local disaster management, mitigation, and education programs; hazards research; political and policy developments; new information sources and Web sites; upcoming conferences; and recent publications. Distributed to over 15,000 subscribers in the United States and abroad via printed copies on their Web site, it focuses on news regarding human adaptation and response to natural hazards and other catastrophic events and provides a forum for concerned individuals to express opinions and generate new ideas through invited personal articles.

United States Geological Survey, hazards research. Available online. URL: http://www.usgs.gov/themes/hazard.html. Accessed May 23, 2007. This Web site has descriptions of many geological hazards, with pages on landslide hazards (Fact Sheet FS-0071-00) and downslope flow hazards. In the United States each year, natural hazards cause hundreds of deaths and cost tens of billions of dollars in disaster aid, disruption of commerce, and destruction of homes and critical infrastructure. This series of Web pages was designed to educate citizens, emergency managers, and lawmakers on seven natural hazards facing the nation—earthquakes, floods, hurricanes, landslides, tsunamis, volcanoes, and wildfires—and show how USGS science helps mitigate disasters and build resilient communities.

Index

Note: Page numbers in *italic* refer to illustrations, *m* indicates a map, *t* indicates a table.

DATE DUE

APR 2 2 2009	

MAY '08